A DYNAMIC GOD

A DYNAMIC GOD

Living an Unconventional
Catholic Faith

Nancy Mairs

BEACON PRESS • BOSTON

Beacon Press
25 Beacon Street
Boston, Massachusetts 02108–2892
www.beacon.org

Beacon Press books
are published under the auspices of
the Unitarian Universalist Association of Congregations.

10 09 08 07   8 7 6 5 4 3 2 1

This book is printed on acid-free paper that meets
the uncoated paper ANSI/NISO specifications
for permanence as revised in 1992.

Text design and composition by
Wilsted & Taylor Publishing Services

Library of Congress Cataloging-in-Publication Data
Mairs, Nancy
A dynamic God : living an unconventional Catholic faith / Nancy Mairs.
p. cm.
ISBN 978-0-8070-7732-0
1. Mairs, Nancy, 1943– 2. Catholics—Biography.
3. Spiritual biography. I. Title.

BX4705.M263129A3 2007
282.092—dc22
[B]   2007013301

"Coveting the Saints: Our Lady of Guadalupe and
the Soup" appeared in different form in A Tremor of Bliss:
Contemporary Writers on the Saints, edited by Paul Elie
(New York: Harcourt Brace, 1994).

For Colin, Trevor, and Molly

intimations of immortality

CONTENTS

FIRST WORDS

Hearken with your ears to these best counsels,
Reflect upon them with illumined judgment.
Let each one choose his creed with that freedom of choice
each must have at great events.
O ye, be awake to these, my announcements.

GATHAS OF ZARATHUSHTRA
(Yasna 30:2), circa 1700 BCE

As my husband and I wound up out of the Salt River canyon on the way from Tucson to Zuni, New Mexico, I found myself thinking about an Afghan woman. Not one particular Afghan woman, because I didn't know any then, but my hypothetical counterpart living under Taliban rule. I don't know why she flitted into my consciousness. It was August 2001, the shattering events that would come to be known as 9/11 still three weeks away, and the general public had not yet uttered the word "Afghanistan," although it was mentioned from time to time in the *New York Times* and on National Public Radio. But I had received via e-mail, at least a dozen times, a petition detailing the plight of the women there, shrouded in burqas, immured in their houses, beaten and stoned for revealing an inch of a wrist if they venture out to market. Since I do not drive and have never been able to read in a car, on long trips my mind lies open to any idea that strays into it. That day I was haunted by an Afghan woman.

I was traveling over paved roads in the front of a minivan

equipped with a ramp and a tie-down for my power wheelchair, from which I watched the canyon's castellated rock formations against an azure sky. It had been a summer of discouragingly little rain, as the landscape's parched and tawny tone reflected. Since my diet does not depend on the squash and corn and beans that can be scratched out of dusty earth, however, the drought raised the threat of fire in the Tonto National Forest we were traversing but not the threat of starvation. We were on our way to visit our daughter and her husband and their three little children, who had just moved to be near Eric's new job with the Indian Health Service. I was not worried that the baby had lost weight since we saw her in June. I didn't fear that one of the boys might have stepped on a land mine and lost a leg in the explosion. As far as I could tell from preliminary reports, the biggest problem the family had encountered so far was fearsome itching from the attacks of a bumper crop of ravenous mosquitoes—and I was not even concerned that these might infect one of us with malaria. Unlike my Afghan counterpart, I have always lived in a state of ease bordering on bliss.

Why should I be this woman and not that one? If I believed in reincarnation, I might view my privileged life as the fruit of some previous virtuous existence and even imagine myself close to leaping off the wheel altogether; but I don't. I don't think that any amount of goodness, in this or any other life, could have merited the joy I feel, any more than her badness could have earned her misery. I am just as bad as she, and she just as good as I, I imagine, and our fates have little to do with our deserts. I happened to get formed out of the gametes of a couple of staunch young Congregationalists, firm practitioners of personal hygiene, higher education, and the Republican vote, in the middle of the last century, whereas she was formed, by the identical process, on the other side of the world and born into a tribal Muslim society in which she would possess little but reproductive value. No great design here. No reward or punishment. Just the random replication of DNA, here or there. The desert we had just traversed, the cliffs past which we climbed, the pine forest and the mesas to come, instructed me to rejoice at my gratuitous good fortune, to grieve for the Afghan woman's scars and starvation.

I would recall these reflections months later, on the first Sunday in Advent, when I was trying to make sense of the Gospel, to make the Gospel sensible to my life, which is my struggle each week throughout the liturgical year. The exact opposite of an inerrantist, I do not believe that the Holy Scriptures serve to instruct me in a Truth handed down once for all time by an adamantine deity. Instead, I have come to view them as a tool, a rigorous and recurrent challenge to unfold truths about the lively Holiness that acts in and upon my life. Each time a reading comes round again, as it will every three years, I can't just receive it, I must engage with it, let it work on me, until it reveals its significance, not to all people everywhere for all time but for me right here, right now, or fails to ring true and spurs me to explore alternatives. In this way, although the words remain constant, each passage may yield fresh insight every time it recurs.

That year, unlike any other since my conversion to Catholicism, I was reading in a time of war. The Afghan woman whose imagined hardships aroused my gratitude for my own good life six summers ago may now—through no fault of her own—very well be dead at the hands of warriors acting on my behalf; as luck would have it, when warriors acting on her behalf attacked, I was far from the Pentagon and the World Trade Center. One of us might have died, the other did not. The risks of war are no less random and reasonless than the rest of the world's individual events. What response, short of lethargy or even downright nihilism, can such bleak knowledge invite? The Advent message: Awake! Live in full awareness of the moment. Because we cannot know the nature of the next mo-

ment, we had better cherish this one. And now this one. This one.
And this.

The gospel according to Nancy.

I am doubtless changed by every book I write. I accumulate information, sometimes quite odd bits of it. Who knew that "sin" comes
from a Greek word used in archery and has nothing to do with fruit
or nakedness or bodies bloodied for our sake? I sift and reexamine
old insights, my own and others', discarding, modifying, reaffirm-
ing. Above all, I explore the familiar elements of my life and grope
toward new ways of understanding them, a process as contemptuous
of logic as the old lady in E. M. Forster's anecdote who expostulates:
"How can I tell what I think till I see what I say?" By the end, I know
more, and differently, than I did before starting. I've never found a
better incentive for writing.

The alteration caused by writing this book is of another order. I
am not at all the woman I was at the outset. I don't mean that I've
had any sort of Extreme Makeover. If you had met me ten years
ago and saw me again today, you'd find me pudgier and wrinklier,
but I think you'd recognize me. Nor have I transformed into a woo-
woo and floated off into spiritual inner or outer space. What I have
undergone is what theologians call "metanoia," which I had always
thought of, insofar as I thought of it at all, as a synonym for the
sort of once-for-all conversion I had made in 1977 when I became
a Roman Catholic. Metanoia, a Greek word meaning a change of
mind, seemed straightforward enough. I knew that for some Christians metanoia signified repentance, which I did constantly, and acceptance of Jesus Christ as one's personal savior, which I had never
done. Beyond that, the word was Greek to me. I never imagined myself to be suffering "a sea-change / Into something rich and strange."
All right, strange maybe. But I wasn't aware of the ongoing radical
revision and transformation that placed the Holy at the center of my
being.

In fact, I wasn't conscious of how differently I live in the world now until a few weeks ago, when out of the blue I said to George, "You know, I'm not worried about this book, not anymore." Suddenly I recognized that an undertone of anxiety has always niggled me right from the start of any project—not just the familiar wild panicked certainty that I couldn't possibly write anything at all *this* time but a subtler and even more debilitating sense that I was not entitled to speak on any subject in which I held no academic credentials, especially now that, unable any longer to hold a book, I had to rely on the Internet for research. (You can find some mighty queer things on the Internet.) This sense of inadequacy was most problematic when I addressed theological matters. I didn't worry about God's reaction to my ruminations, but I dreaded human rejection and ridicule.

And then the strife was over. I no longer worried whether I was entitled to speak about the Holy. The Church (by which I mean, here and hereafter, the institutional Roman Catholic Church) might accuse me of heresy and excommunicate me (as apparently they have done because of my affiliation with the reformist group Call to Action), but they couldn't thereby separate me from God, who was my marrow. If I needed spiritual nourishment, I could take Communion anywhere, even anonymously the Catholic Eucharist. What were they going to do, hire somebody to trail around after me and leap in my path if I headed for a church door? Because this book intended to reveal an evolving faith in a dynamic God through a radical rereading of many of the conventional doctrines of Christianity, I knew from the start it was a risky business. Secular humanists might reject it as a "religious" book. Traditional Catholics seemed likely to characterize me as a cafeteria Catholic, at the least, even a heretic or an apostate. (Technically, I think I am all these.) Fundamentalists, both Catholic and Protestant, might condemn it as the work of the devil. (It is not.) Academics might dismiss me because I am not a scholar. Good Lord, who's left? Actually, many people I meet seem eager to contemplate spiritual matters without necessarily committing themselves to a specific religious tradition, or with reservations about the tradition they espouse. I decided to throw my lot in with them.

Although I am no biblical literalist, I had always thought I had to account somehow for every passage of the Gospels, to puzzle out the truth hidden in even the most obscure or offensive phrase. But my energies were more productively spent, I learned as I wrote, puzzling out God Godself and attending to the passages true to God's message of (sometimes very tough) love. Like Amos, "I was no prophet, nor have I belonged to a company of prophets" (Amos 7:14), as long as I thought of prophecy as a sort of fortune-telling, but once I understood it as plain talk about the presence of God in everyday life, what else could I do but prophesy, in the sense not of preaching or predicting but of bearing witness to God-with-us, Emmanuel.[1]

My life is immersed in issues of social justice, actions to promote peace, ethical contemplation, celebration of the glories of creation. What am I going to write about—the Red Sox? (I could do so, and with considerable expertise, but I don't think I could commit myself to the work for any length of time. Some things matter, and some don't, though I doubt I could sway all Red Sox fans to include the object of their obsession in the latter category.) My task is to address spiritual concerns truthfully in a manner neither didactic nor sanctimonious nor airy fairy. I don't have to please the critics or clerics or scholars. I don't even have to please God. Nor do I plan to proselytize, since your conversion to my faith is a matter of indifference both to me and to God. If you can undertake to love All, I'm not the one to direct you as to the means you choose. I'm here to learn.

But first to unlearn. I've found myself descending more and more deeply into a state of radical uncertainty, or learned ignorance, to use Nicholas of Cusa's term. I don't mean I've lost my mind. I know a hawk from a handsaw in all weathers. I am as capable of acquiring information and of reasoning closely about it as anyone else thoroughly trained in feminist and psychoanalytic theory who has engaged in literary analysis for the better part of her life, but the project I've undertaken here, though cerebral, is not a reasonable one. God is not a rational concept susceptible of proof, and so belief in God is the product of inspired choice or madness, depending on your point of view.

I've never understood why the unreasonableness of believing in God should preclude God's existence to rational minds. The human psyche can certainly encompass both rational thought and wild imagination. Perhaps what holds the logical mind back here as in so many other instances is fear of the uncertainty upon which faith rests precariously, uneasily, as though in a quaking bog, so different from cold, hard facts. I now know that I now know less about God than I did to begin with. I have discarded as many fixed ideas as possible about the God I inherited, and I'm unlearning more every day. My mind must be emptied ceaselessly, since it fills up, faster than a litter bin on a busy street, with rigid precepts and preconceptions which create a clatter that no still, small voice could possibly penetrate.

The essays that follow represent some of the insights that have emerged from this deconstructive process. They are indeed "essays," just as Michel de Montaigne coined the literary term, "trials" of my responses to living in God's presence, not chapters in an extended didactic or argumentative work. In them I use the words "God," "the Holy One" or "the Holy," "the Whole," "the All," and various words from other traditions, none of which reflect the smallest part of what I mean, let alone what I am incapable of knowing and meaning.

In this book I function rather like one of the Hebrew and Christian Scriptures' wilder prophetic figures, Jesus's cousin John the Baptist. I don't relish this role. Does anyone? Did John himself?

It's not the locusts I'd mind so much. My daughter, who lived in Africa for some years, reports that even if they're cooked in palm oil with onion, garlic, tomatoes, and hot red peppers, they still look like locusts, and the legs scratch on the way down; even so, I could probably swallow them to stave off starvation. But who wants to be a voice crying in the wilderness? Sweeter by far to sing in concert, your voice just one strand in the weave of music—and if you wander a little off key, the others will cover you, no one will hear your gaffe, no one will snicker, accuse you of showing off, dismiss you for stridency. I've never wanted to play Antigone or Medea. Let me be one voice in the wise and distant Greek chorus any day.

But what if, like John, you possess a piece of knowledge so extraordinary that you know it could—if believed—change the world forever? He couldn't very well keep silent once he understood that God's arrival was imminent, that all anyone had to do was clear the heart's path and God would stride right in. He had to shout out the news, break into whatever despair or smugness or distraction choked the way like weeds, make people ready to receive the Holy. And each of us has to do the same, reach out to others in gesture and word, sustaining each other in our perennial task of following the truths we have discovered (not received—nothing easy like that) every day. Because God doesn't saunter in once for all and settle like a large cat plumping herself into your favorite rocker with an air that says, "Here I am! Now your life is complete!" God dances beyond the threshold and must continually be enticed into our dwelling. I hope these essays remind us all to extend that invitation, clean all the corners and polish the windows, throw wide the door.

PART I

WHY I AM THE CATHOLIC I AM: A JOURNEY

LEFT AT THE ALTAR

*Sakka asked the Buddha: "Do different religious
teachers head for the same goal or practice the
same disciplines or aspire to the same thing?"*

*"No, Sakka, they do not. And why? This world is
made up of myriad different states of being, and people
adhere to one or another of these states and become
tenaciously possessive of them, saying, 'This alone is
true, everything else is false.' It is like a territory that
they believe is theirs. So all religious teachers do
not teach the same goal or the same discipline,
nor do they aspire to the same thing.*

*"But if you find truth in any religion or philosophy,
then accept that truth without prejudice."*

DIGHA NIKAYA

A few months ago, during the question-and-answer period following one of my readings, a woman prefaced her question, "Since
you were once a Catholic..." Although I remained motionless, in-
wardly I jumped in startlement. I *am* a Catholic. That is how I identify myself, even though I recognize that the regime in Rome would
not agree with me. Most of them are not converts, however, and so
they can never share the sense I had upon declaring my Catholicism that I had come home. I was where I belonged. I still have that
feeling when I enter a church, bless myself with holy water, light

a candle, and pray. These little rituals have no intrinsic meaning for me but they do possess an inarticulable worth that makes them more than empty gestures.

Since my conversion, I have gone to a religious service most weeks; I now worship with a small community dedicated to peace and justice. Through this affiliation, which has come to animate my faith and principles moment by moment, I have grown uneasy with the label "Christian." I suspected from the outset that I wasn't a "real" Catholic, not in the Roman sense, and I have become more than content to call myself an alternative Catholic or a Zen Catholic. But I still thought of myself as a Christian. Gradually, however, I began to see that "the Christ" referred not so much to an entity as to an accretion of ideas, formed across centuries, largely by men, many of whom appeared to suffer from considerable sexual anxiety, and imposed systematically, often by intimidation, upon various populations (among them my own gender), not all of whom benefited from their espousal. This setup sounded to me more descriptive of the Romans than the Christians.

Truth to tell, I recognize now, the meanings commonly ascribed to Christianity entail an accumulation of beliefs, some of which I simply cannot embrace. If belief in personal salvation defines a Christian, for instance, then I do not call myself one. How, then, to identify myself? Perhaps the term "pre-Christian" is as descriptive as any other, harking back to the earliest days after Jesus's execution, when his followers gathered over simple meals, bread and wine and perhaps a little fish, and recollected his words as best they could. Over time, others joined them, who had to be told his story, who had to be taught his precepts, and one can easily understand how tellers might blur some details, elaborate others, add some to suit the needs of a particular audience for comfort, discipline, excitement, mystery. Gradually, to suit the inclinations of his followers, Jesus became less a rabbinical figure than a messianic or a mystical one. But I remain drawn to the Teacher.

Because I'm not a biblical scholar, I look to *The Five Gospels* of the Jesus Seminar and the reconstructed Q sayings[1]—documents that emerged out of the tremendous growth in knowledge in the twentieth century about the early Christian church—to reveal what an itinerant Jewish teacher on fire with a vision of a transformed reality might have said to his followers, both then and today. (Now there's a leap of faith for you: relying on a text that doesn't even exist! The hypothetical Q sayings comprise material upon which Matthew and Luke are thought to have drawn for their Gospels.) "What is remarkable about Q1 [the first section of the Q sayings]," according to one author,

> is that the original Christians appeared to be centered totally on concerns about their relationships with God and with other people, and their preparation for the imminent arrival of Kingdom of God on earth. Totally absent from their spiritual life are almost all of the factors that we associate with Christianity today. There is *absolutely no mention* of (in alphabetic order): adultery, angels, apostles, baptism, church, clergy, confirmation, crucifixion, demons, disciples, divorce, Eucharist, great commission to convert the world, healing, heaven, hell, incarnation, infancy stories, John the Baptist, Last Supper, life after death, Mary and Joseph and the rest of Jesus' family, magi, miracles, Jewish laws concerning behavior, marriage, Messiah, restrictions on sexual behavior, resurrection, roles of men and women, Sabbath, salvation, Satan, second coming, signs of the end of the age, sin, speaking in tongues, temple, tomb, transfiguration, trial of Jesus, trinity, or the virgin birth.[2]

Although a number of the elements mentioned here are dear to me, and a few figure deeply in my spiritual life, none contribute essentially to my understanding of the Holy. Like the "original Christians" (who probably would not have thought of themselves in those words), I focus on putting myself in right relationship with God and God's creatures in order to bring about the Kindom of God[3] *on earth*, which is the only place where I can be certain that it might exist. Whether or not there is a sweet hereafter I'll find out in the sweet hereafter. Because no evidence of a life to come has ever been found, belief in it requires a pure leap of faith that my skeptical nature cannot make. Indeed, I suspect that the reason we don't know what happens to us after death is that nothing—nothing, at least, that we can conceive—happens. No matter. For the time being, my task is to realize, moment by moment, the sweet now.

In the light of all that I've just said, you might well ask, as I do almost daily, why I identify with Catholicism, whose leaders would, if they knew I existed, straightaway pitch me out, a religion notorious for its moral violence against women, its abuse of clerical power, its use of fear to keep its practitioners compliant—oh, don't get me going! Any reply I can make falls outside the boundaries of reason and so cannot be understood but only received or rejected according to one's tolerance for the absurd. Simply put, I apprehend all creation as sacred, and Catholicism has provided me the symbols and ceremonies for recognizing, contemplating, celebrating the Holy.

I write these words at the start of Advent, the fourth Sunday before Christmas, the beginning both of the liturgical year and of the Christmas season, which will last until Epiphany on January 6. I love the Christmas story, with its mélange of stars and angels, the pregnancies of an unmarried girl and an elderly woman, rough shepherds and rich magi bearing an odd assortment of gifts for a newborn (including a substance used in embalming), even a wicked king—enough elements to construct an account of epic proportions, just as the authors of the Gospels of Matthew and Luke (a woman?[4]) did, creating tales of such power that they have endured (with considerable elaboration) from the latter part of the first century CE until today. This is not the only infancy narrative in the world's richly various mythologies involving a miraculous birth, and certainly not the oldest, but it must be one of the most widespread and tenacious. The origins of all life, especially our own, mystify us. Even scientists have yet to discover why a pregnant woman's immune system does not reject and destroy the foreign tissue of the placenta and fetus as it would harmful bacteria. But even after the mechanics of the matter have been explained, its essence remains mysterious. You can no more know what you were before you than you can know what will become of you after. Only stories can capture the miracle of being born at all, and the birth of a cultural god or hero lends itself especially well to mythmaking. Matthew and Luke drew heavily on the stories that had proliferated in the decades following Jesus's death, as well as other culturally current sources. They both relied on Mark, and Matthew, a Jew, on Hebrew Scripture as well. Thus, they had rich materials out of which to shape their accounts.

I have not believed in many years that the miraculous events in the Gospels actually happened, nor must I in order to "live" the myth of the Christmas story. Unfortunately, many people equate "myth" with "untruth," but myths often lead us into deeper truths than facts can. Advent and Christmas remind me to contemplate them. The Annunciation teaches me that I can bear gracefully the random and sometimes astonishing events that shape my life. The Advent readings urge me to "stay awake and watch," ready for the manifestations of the Holy that burst upon me. In the birth itself, with all its signs and wonders, the figure of Jesus affirms that we are at once human and divine, each one a tiny fragment of the All—and we had best behave accordingly.

Because my daughter and her husband hold an adamantly secular view of life yet agree that their children need familiarity with the myths that make up human culture, they have allowed George and me, as the only practicing Christians in the family, to introduce Colin, Trevor, and Molly to the basic stories in the Judeo-Christian tradition. This is hardly an onerous task, since their expectations are minimal, along the lines of being able to distinguish a church from a castle, and we have fun browsing beautifully illustrated books recounting the creation, the flood, the Nativity, which will later resonate with similar tales from other cultures, thereby offering the children an overarching view of some of the fundamental truths of human reality.

One Christmas we bought them a *nacimiento*, since Christianity, among many other systems developed to account for the mystery of human presence in the universe, begins (like all life) with a miraculous birth. We bought a painted ceramic set made in Mexico: good-sized, representational figures with brown faces and gaily colored garments, housed in a stable of wood and straw. Since Colin had gone to a Lutheran preschool the year before and was attending a Catholic one this year, he identified Jesus right away.

"We'd like to tell you a story about them," we said after he and Trevor had unwrapped all the pieces (Molly cheerfully munching on the discarded bits of paper), so we all gathered around the dining table while I narrated and George introduced the characters in their turn. "It's the story of Jesus's birthday."

"Happy buffday to you, happy buffday to you!" they sang out, Colin tunelessly, Trevor right on key.

"Shh, shh, listen now," said their mother, and I told them about the man named Joseph and the woman named Mary, traveling to a village far, far away, whose baby was born unexpectedly among the animals in a barn because they couldn't find a hotel room to stay in. When I got to the part about the shepherds (represented by a boy whose head would be knocked off during Advent but safely reattached with a drop of Elmer's glue), the angel suddenly caroled— not "Gloria in excelsis Deo!" as I had planned but the birthday song. "Happy birthday, baby Jesus!" I trilled as George wafted the boy and his silly sheep through the air to kneel beside the infant, who had kicked off his swaddling clothes, in his manger, and the boys clapped.

"The angel sang"—here swooped in the angel to perch atop the stable—"to tell them how glad God was that Jesus had been born. And every time a baby is born, if you listen very quietly, you can hear an angel sing. One sang when you were born," I said, looking into Colin's solemn eyes. "And one sang when you were born," I said to Trevor's beaming gaze. "And of course one sang for Molly." She was nursing noisily.

I finished up with the kings, who lumbered in on their camels, their precious gifts hugged against their chests, and duly pronounced, "The End," but I had made the point of the story already, a point I hadn't known I was going to make at the outset, a point I hadn't even fully recognized until the angel burst into unexpected song. A people celebrates the birth of the Holy Child not for its singularity but for its universal significance: The Holy has come into the world. With the birth of every infant, the Holy comes anew. God rejoices time after time.

Could I otherwise achieve these insights and the many others this tale has yielded and will yield each time it comes around? I assume so. Unlike myriad others who profess religious belief and practice its rituals, I do not believe that the Almighty has conferred upon me and my kind, and withheld from everyone else, privileged knowledge, which can be used to gain material and spiritual benefits in this world and eternal bliss in the next. That is a tale every bit as fanciful as the Christmas story but it leads the spirit in a very different direction, diminishing the All to a possessible deity and thus making no theological sense whatsoever. God cannot be any smaller than God is.

For years after my conversion, I attended Mass once a week in relative tranquility. To be sure, I had to profess some preposterous beliefs that I couldn't hold, at least not in the way the bishops in Nicaea probably had in mind, but I figured the problem was mine, not God's. I had joined the Church after Vatican II, during the Prague Spring of Roman Catholicism, after teaching in a Catholic high school alongside sisters whose social activism surpassed any I'd yet experienced. They used to spend their summers working with the farm workers in California, getting arrested with the farm workers, going to jail with the farm workers, and in the fall they'd regale us with tales of what they did on their summer vacation. I attended the Newman Center at the University of Arizona, where women served as lectors, Eucharistic ministers, even homilists—but never, of course, celebrants. It was that "of course" that began to disturb my peace.

For a while, the possibility that the Vatican would respond to multiple petitions by authorizing women's ordination had seemed improbable but not altogether fantastical, but in 1994 Pope John II destroyed that hope (though not infallibly) by pronouncing: "Wherefore, in order that all doubt may be removed regarding a matter of great importance, a matter which pertains to the Church's divine constitution itself, in virtue of my ministry of confirming the brethren (cf. Lk 22:32) I declare that the Church has no authority whatsoever to confer priestly ordination on women and that this judgment is to be definitively held by all the Church's faithful" because of "the example recorded in the Sacred Scriptures of Christ choosing his Apostles only from among men; the constant practice of the Church, which has imitated Christ in choosing only men; and her living teaching authority which has consistently held that the exclusion of women from the priesthood is in accordance with God's plan for his Church."[5] In short, we holy men got hold of the story right away, before most women were literate, and told it the way we wanted, we have always told it that way, and (arrogance upon arrogance) God wants us to tell it that way forever.

By then, I had pretty much given up on ordination anyway, having observed that the power of forgiving sins and creating the substance that bestows salvation could lead to self-importance and a sense of immunity from the claims of the mundane world. (Just how right I was I wouldn't learn until the issues of sexual molestation by priests and ecclesial cover-up began to draw public attention in the 1990s.) Why visit upon women too the risks that unchecked power often entails? Safer for the souls of all us believers to take literally the radically democratic phrase "priesthood of the people," recognize that we are by virtue of our existence, with or without our assent, consecrated to the Holy, and accept our sacerdotal lot.

Nearly twenty years ago, talking with Nancy Carroll, a woman I admired for her work with my husband on *¡Presente!*, a newsletter put out in the 1980s by Tucson's Catholics for Peace and Justice, I mentioned feeling troubled that only an ordained man could say the words that turn wheat and grapes, oldest and most basic of sustenance, into Something Else. The imprecision of this phrase gets at the way the Church has arrogated power to itself by persuading the faithful that the ingestion of a numinous substance will save them from a hell of the Church's own devising and that such a substance can be obtained only at the hands of a limited population of celibate males whom the Church consecrates for the task: a kind of centuries-old mystification racket. Not that I believe that most of the men who celebrate Mass conduct a cynical grab for power. On the contrary, they act in deadly earnest. At a conference, I remember a young priest expressing terror at the possibility that a non-Catholic might slip past and receive the host from his hands, causing him to commit an abomination. "Good grief," I said, "what do you think will happen to the host if it falls into the wrong mouth? Don't you think that God can take care of Godself?" Apparently not, and the responsibility for God's purity weighed heavily.

Something does happen during the liturgy of the Eucharist, but the transformation occurs not in the bread and wine, which stubbornly remain themselves, real food and drink, outward and visible signs of inward and spiritual grace, in the words of the Book of Common Prayer. What changes in the course of Holy Communion is not these elements but the communicant, whose body is nourished, if only infinitesimally, by them, and whose spirit is strengthened and sustained by the awareness once again of taking God in in preparation for living God out.

"You should come to the service I've been attending," my friend urged me more than once. And so one day George and I drove into the Tucson Mountains, down a narrow dirt road posted NO HUNTING EXCEPT FOR PEACE, to the small manufactured building that housed the chapel of the Desert House of Prayer, a center for contemplative prayer established and staffed by the Redemptorists. There, Father Ricardo Elford, himself a Redemptorist and one of the earliest members of the Sanctuary Movement founded by Quaker Jim Corbett and Presbyterian John Fife, conducted Mass for a small gathering of peace and justice activists. George and I were not directly involved in Sanctuary, which began in the 1980s in response to growing numbers of Central American refugees seeking political asylum from widespread "disappearing," torture, and death at the hands of the military (many of whose officers had been trained in the United States). That is, we did not ourselves smuggle and shelter the refugees as did Bernie Muller, who would drive her truck close to the border and set up her easel and paints so that if La Migra came along, they would see a white-haired artist sketching the glorious Sonoran Desert (in which thousands of cross-border migrants have died). When her passengers arrived, she stowed them along with her art supplies and drove them to Tucson. There, an underground railroad passed many of them along as far away as Canada. Those who remained in Tucson have been served by Sanctuary's outgrowth, the Center for Prevention and Resolution of Violence, funded by the Hopi Foundation to provide medical care and counseling for survivors of torture.

George and I played only a supportive role, attending vigils and actions, one of which led to our arrest for peacefully occupying our congressman's office, the charges for which were soon dropped. This was a far milder outcome than the five years in prison and $10,000 fines faced by an ecumenical group of eleven, including two Roman Catholic priests and a nun, who in 1985 were tried in Tucson on charges of conspiring to transport and shelter Central American "aliens." The defendants believed in the legality and moral imperative of giving sanctuary to people genuinely in fear for their lives, who should be granted temporary refugee status under the 1980 Refugee Act. Eight of the accused were convicted and placed on probation. We have more recently been involved with Owl and Panther, a group of torture survivors ranging in age from six to adult from countries including Mauritania, Mali, Uganda, Guatemala, El Salvador, Honduras, and Mexico, who write poetry as a means of healing their terror and homesickness. I cannot resist including one of my favorite poems, by Wendy Salazar Jimenez from Guatemala:

> *Ask me about war and killing*
> *Ask me about torture and fear*
> *Ask me about hate and hunger*
> *Ask me about my childhood*
> *Ask me about my hopes and dreams*
> *But don't ask me about happiness yet*[6]

Wendy's family now owns a terrific Guatemalan restaurant, one wall of which bears a huge mural painted by Bernie Muller. Wendy, now a pretty and lively young woman trained as an LPN, works at a Tucson hospital while studying to become an RN. One day I may ask her about happiness, but not yet.

I don't even remember the first day George and I worshiped with the activists from the Sanctuary Movement, and I'm sure I didn't know that it would alter my life at all, let alone unfathomably and forever. I do remember that, the first few times we attended, I felt awkward sitting in a circle and singing and praying aloud without a large congregation in which to hide my voice. I also remember my delight that Marguerite Reed, a Presbyterian minister, assisted Ricardo, although in those days she may not have uttered the Eucharistic Prayer. Since Ricardo always placed on the altar an icon by Robert Lentz titled *Christ of the Desert*, we came to call ourselves Community of Christ of the Desert. This icon, from the Syriac tradition of Christianity, shows Jesus as a vigorous young Semite, his face framed by a pure white robe and his hands raised in a gesture of blessing or surrender—a clear contrast to the pale, blue-eyed figure clutching his bleeding heart which decorates many a Catholic home.

Almost too gradually to notice, George and I shifted our weekly worship from the Newman Center to this group. On our twenty-fifth wedding anniversary, Ricardo said the Mass during which we renewed our vows, this time as Catholics. When George had a six-centimeter melanoma removed from his belly, Ricardo brought him Communion each of the ten days he was in hospital, and members of the Community ferried us to and from chemotherapy treatments. Since the rest of our family don't practice any religion, the Community serves as our spiritual home. "Are your children coming for Easter?" one of them once asked me. "Certainly not!" I laughed, trying to imagine my daughter, an adamant secularist, participating in any of the rituals we perform at that time. She's a whiz at playing Easter bunny, as she is at every activity that involves her children, but I think it best to leave crucifixion out of the paschal picture. "When it comes to religion, you are our family."

From the outset, our members were not traditional Catholics (or necessarily, after a while, Catholics at all). Although we were not poor ourselves, we adhered to the statement made by the Latin American bishops when they convened in 1979 in Puebla, Mexico:

"We affirm the need for conversion on the part of the whole Church to a preferential option for the poor, an option aimed at their eternal liberation."[7] In accordance with this theological tenet, we modeled ourselves on the Christian base communities that emerged in Latin America in the last third of the twentieth century: small groups of lay people who together studied the Bible as it illuminates the realities of everyday life and put their insights into practices designed to transform society. Functioning outside the Church hierarchy, these groups and the liberation theology on which they were based were already under strenuous attack by the Vatican by the time we came together.

Thus, we knew we would never receive the Church's approval of our Community, and we have never sought it. Like a giant snail that pokes its tentacles into the air and, if startled, pulls back into calcified coils and seals itself in darkness, the Church seemed about to transcend the injustices built into its structure but then retreated, abruptly and absolutely, into the arguments and practices that had immured it in sin for centuries. Those of us who thrived on the creative energy that followed Vatican II have not left the Church; rather, the Church has left us twisting in the winds of change, of uncertainty, of new life. We work to propel the movement abandoned by the Church: making real the Kindom of God here, now, as promised by the Jesus of the Gospels.

We began to hold our celebration, followed by a potluck dinner, in one another's homes, at first intermittently, then regularly. On one of these occasions, I voiced the qualm that had drawn me into this group in the first place. "Ricardo, I'm sick of whispering the Eucharistic Prayer along with you," I said. "I want to speak aloud. I want to say the Mass."

"Well, you should do something about that," he replied. Instead of defending or executing the special powers of ordination, he handed the matter back to me; I was the one with the problem, not he. After some reflection and conversation with other members, I proposed to the Community that we recite the Eucharistic Prayer together, in keeping with our belief in a true priesthood of the people. Some stipulated that an ordained priest would have to participate ("really" effecting the salvific transformation while the rest of us just recited the words with him), but that seemed acceptable: my purpose, after all, was not to stop Ricardo from saying the words but to add my voice to his. We continued to use the Catholic liturgy, although we'd begun to take in people unsatisfied by other traditions, among them Presbyterian, United Church of Christ, Quaker, and Buddhist. We might incorporate nonscriptural readings—from Oscar Romero or Dorothy Day, for instance—but we always read from the Gospels, even if the passage horrifies us, and tussle with it during the dialogue with which we have replaced the homily. The tone of our discussions is not doctrinaire but interrogative. We do not promulgate a set of beliefs to which all must adhere on penalty of death and damnation. We are not so sure. Rather, we struggle to form, clarify, and articulate our beliefs—or even, sometimes, to hold any at all.

During the years we all recited the Eucharistic Prayer, we kept our practices to ourselves because we knew full well that, though acceptable to God, they were expressly forbidden by the Catholic Church. None of us cared to take on that institution. One night, when one of our newer members asked why we didn't all sign a newspaper advertisement protesting the Iraq war as Community of Christ of the Desert instead of signing one by one, I said, referring to the gathering places of early Christians, "Do you remember the catacombs?" She nodded. "Well, that's where we are." There was general laughter, since we were clearly sitting in Cindy and Leo's bright living room as the evening darkened outside the open front door, but we knew I wasn't merely joking. We knew full well that we wouldn't be thrown into the Colosseum with gladiators or lions. The Romans arrayed against us were Christians, after all, not pagans. Nevertheless, they could cause unpleasant upheavals in our lives of service and worship.

The one who had to worry the most was Ricardo, since he would be held responsible, by virtue of ordination, not merely for the spiritual well-being of all of us but, more important from an ecclesial point of view, the defense of priestly privilege. I think he always worried about discovery, the more so as the Church became more repressive, stripping Charles Curran of the right to teach theology in a Church university and dismissing Matthew Fox from the Dominican Order. In Tucson, a new bishop made clear that priests were not to deviate by one kiss of peace from the Vatican's instructions. Finally, Ricardo told us one night that he could not go on: "I just can't face showing up on the front page of *National Catholic Reporter*," as he probably would do if Bishop Kicanas chose to make him an example of a renegade priest. I was appalled, and I'm sure I wasn't alone. Some of us had worried that the obligation he felt to be with us every Saturday evening, on top of all his ministry to the Yaqui, refugee, and poor Latino families on the South Side, would overburden him, but this fear of exposure seemed much more onerous. "I think there are a couple of options," Ricardo suggested. "We could go back to the way we were, with me saying the Eucharistic Prayer alone. Or we could change to a bread-breaking service, not using the precise words of the Eucharistic Prayer. Think about it and let me know what you want."

I could accept either choice as long as the Community survived. The law against utterance of a few phrases by lay lips now seemed silly to me, a stricture to be not transgressed but dismissed. I was and I remain confident that Jesus is present in whatever form our worship takes, true to his word: "Where two or three are gathered together in my name, there am I in the midst of them" (Matt. 18:20). He does not require a particular set of words or gestures in order to come among us, although some of us do require them in order to discern Jesus's real presence and so must go to "real" Mass the next morning. I believe that the meal we partake of is consecrated, that Jesus has come among us, mysteriously and miraculously, in our very gathering at the table, and I don't much mind what words are spoken about it and who speaks them. Others must have thought along similar lines, because the Community remained virtually intact during our transformation from a Eucharistic to a eucharistic community, one that eats bread and drinks wine together in order to give thanks for our blessings and gain strength to do God's work in the world. We are Church.[8]

I live in a church. Not that you'd know to look at it. It has no stained glass, no belfry (other than the one I have bats in). A small Craftsman-style reproduction in a new "green" community at the edge of an historic neighborhood, it is, well, pretty. Not dignified. Not grand. The painted tile by the front door and some of the paintings, sculptures, candles, and photographs inside suggest a devotion to Our Lady of Guadalupe, as well as to local artists. On several walls hang crosses from Mexico, Ethiopia, Ireland. To a stranger, it might well resemble the interiors I glimpsed when young on the rare occasions I visited Catholic households, with garishly dressed statuary and those paintings of sad-eyed Jesuses with fiery hearts, reeking of the idolatry that I had been trained to revile. I never understood the intensity of my mother's loathing of Catholicism I've often referred to in my writings, shared to some degree or another by others in my family. It was strong enough that in the letter accepting my father's proposal of marriage, she wrote that nothing could prevent her from marrying him except his being a Catholic, an odd point to bring up in view of his staunch Congregationalism. It never seemed to rub off on me.

Religious artifacts notwithstanding, you wouldn't take the interior of my house for a church either, occupied as it is by a black Labrador retriever and two weirder-than-usual black cats and decorated with the detritus of a literary life. Nevertheless, we bought it with the Community in mind. The bedrooms are awkwardly small, but the social space accommodates thirty-five people for both worship and conviviality. A large coffee table serves as an altar, decorated with flowers and candles and sometimes an icon or photograph, and we have a Papago basket for the bread and a Zuni chalice for the wine. The stereo plays music to accompany our singing. Voilà! A church! A space is made sacred not by solemn and elaborate ceremonies that set it aside from the mundane but by its use for welcoming the Holy, present always and everywhere but unattended in the hustle of our daily lives.

Every few weeks, the transformation occurs again. More and more people arrive, exhausting our motley supply of indoor and outdoor chairs and some borrowed ones as well. As more people, disaffected by their own traditions, hear about us, our numbers swell. We do not recruit, but neither do we want to turn away anyone who needs to be with us, and each new person contributes a different spice to the mix. So we squeeze a little closer, knowing that, as deaths (not uncommon in our aging group) and departures occur, the balance may correct itself before we outgrow even the most spacious homes.

If we become much larger, I suppose we'll have to abandon the house-church model and hire a hall in which to gather. If it has kitchen facilities, we might continue to share a meal after worship. But without the intimacy of a home setting, which invites relaxation and openness, the group's character would certainly change. Perhaps some of us, made uncomfortable by crowding or missing the circle formation that would once again enable us to look into one another's faces, would welcome the new conformation; others would grieve the change as a loss, as I would. With luck, a critical mass of us would have the faith to shift locations and wait to see how we evolve this time.

We retain the shape of the Catholic Mass, but the shift to a bread-breaking service has revitalized our liturgy, which people take turns composing. In recent months we have used prayers and readings from Jewish tradition, Hildegard von Bingen, Gandhi, César Chávez, Tecumseh, and Martin Luther King Jr. We always include a gospel, though not always chosen from the canon; we sing in English, Spanish, and Latin. Our dialogues are always tricky. Even though we agree, when the matter is raised, that this time is most appropriately used for reflection on the readings for the day, because we are deeply committed to issues of peace and social justice, and because our convictions in these matters often diverge from those held by the majority of people who wield various kinds of power, our discussions often veer dangerously in the direction of self-pity: we poor enlightened few, struggling against the benighted masses who take unquestioned direction from the right wing in church and government, lament a litany of social and political ills, each one topping the one before in a dispiriting game of Ain't It Awful—a reductive model based on just the dichotomous thinking we repudiate in our critique of "them."

We voice the same complaints over and over: Bombs are pulverizing the countryside and populations in the Middle East. Distracted by fear of terrorism, the American people are allowing the government to abrogate our civil rights and to heap billions of dollars in tax cuts and rebates on the wealthiest individuals and corporations even as its citizens lose their jobs, their homes, their hope. Cross-border migrants die by the hundreds in the desert. The Church is sliding precipitously back into theological medievalism. The world is, in its habitual fashion, going to hell in a handbasket.

Some of the group clearly believe that if we just spoke a little louder and worked a little harder, we could persuade people to take care of one another and the world, but I do not. Not that I don't embrace these values. I believe in them. I just don't believe that most people will choose to change. The trick is to keep working to resolve issues without having to believe that the world will become a better place as a result. I have learned to do so, but I need a lot of support, and we seem too often mired in a quicksand of woes where I for one am suffocating. "Listen to us," I recall bursting in one night. "I know we need a safe place to say these things, especially now that even a whisper of opposition is considered treasonous, but even if 90 percent support the government's actions, then 10 percent of us don't—and 10 percent is not nothing. We count. Look at tonight's Gospel. In it, John isn't issuing a call to complaint but a call to action. What can we *do?*"

Of all the people I know, the ones in this group are among the most committed activists—tirelessly standing vigil on the eve of every execution, sheltering and counseling refugees, scrubbing pots at Our Lady of Guadalupe Free Kitchen, crossing the line at the Nevada Nuclear Test Site, marching on Fort Benning to protest the School of the Americas, driving trucks loaded with medical supplies to Central America with Pastors for Peace, lugging water to remote stations along the border, and I was immediately ashamed of my Johannine harangue. "I look on this gathering as a refuge," I continued more quietly, "the one time I can gather my scattered wits and focus on the Holy. Could we please turn our discussion back to today's reading?" I've spoken this way more than once. The group accepts my eruption with characteristic grace, and usually the discussion does veer in a more positive direction. Some speak rarely and others frequently. By the end, I always see at least one point in a new light. Always.

At the end of the service, we assemble a groaning board. Everyone contributes a dish. Sometimes the variety of offerings is a little off kilter—one evening, I recall, we ate nothing but dessert—but we have never gone hungry. This is an important part of our gathering. Because we seldom see one another during the week, here we can exchange our own news or news of members who are doing volunteer work in Malawi or China or Guatemala. We deal with grave illness and mourn the loss of members, some to relocation but more to death. When Miriam and Michael fell in love right before our eyes and married, we rejoiced, as we did at the births of Cameron and Lee Ann; when their sister lived only thirty-six hours, we lamented. In short, we function as a family—an unusually amiable one, since we don't live with one another's quirks most of the time!

Coming home after Holy Communion at St. Andrew's, the little Episcopal church two blocks from our home, George commented, "Well, that was very nice, but it seemed... flat." We don't object to going to church-church, and we're apt to do so when the Community can't meet or we can't get there, but even though our spiritual lives differ markedly, neither of us seems much engaged by a conventional service anymore. That form of worship feels somehow static, imposed upon us rather than unfolding out of us. We miss the intimacy of crowding together, the creativity of our liturgy, the surprise and humor that bubble up in our dialogue.

Sometimes people express wistfulness when they learn about our quality of worship, as though we possess something they don't. But although the Community of Christ of the Desert may be rare, it is not—need not be—unique. Indeed, many small faith communities exist throughout the country, but these are generally sponsored by a church or diocese and thus subject to constraints of form and practice that would have curtailed our evolution into the experimental, skeptical, interfaith community we have grown into. As more people become alienated from "religion" of various sorts, with its stony framework of strictures and scripture, new groups may form. Because the Community has evolved, and is likely to continue to do so, we have no blueprint for its design—nor should we. Groups should be free to form their distinctive personalities. The Community can't be replicated, but it can be imitated, and I hope that it will be. It is "like yeast which a woman took and hid in three measures of flour, till it was leavened" (Matt. 13:33). It might not take very many of us to transform our various faiths, breaching the barriers institutions erect, relinquishing requirements that must be defended from or imposed upon others, and clustering, in diverse ways, to celebrate and serve the Holy in all life. As we progress into the unknown, we should call out to one another through the dark. I guess this essay constitutes my first cry. I'm listening.

COVETING THE SAINTS:
OUR LADY OF GUADALUPE
AND THE SOUP

Taking an unfamiliar shortcut through a residential neighborhood on Tucson's west side, my husband screeches to a halt and throws the van into reverse, bobbing me around like one of those dashboard puppies in my wheelchair in the back. "Look at that!" George cries, pulling up beside a mural depicting La Virgen de Guadalupe painted on a hole-in-the-wall grocery, La Tiendita, at the corner of two empty streets. "Isn't that wonderful!" Such wall art is common here, especially in the barrios, and it often features La Guadalupana, as do jewelry, scarves and other articles of clothing, and even the hoods of automobiles. This is a relatively crude production, not signed: the figure faces the wrong direction, and most of the significant details are missing. But she stands upon the head of a truly glorious fanged serpent, painted a violet so intense that it shivers in the opalescent light of an overcast winter day in the desert, surrounded by scowling brown pre-Colombian heads. The overall effect is exuberant and, indeed, wonderful, a treasure stumbled upon in haste.

Perhaps because we're in a hurry, it doesn't occur to me until hours later, as I settle in to begin this essay, that I am, both aesthetically and spiritually, not the woman I used to be. I was certainly brought up to know that the colors in that mural clashed. Except the brown, of course—but oh! those hideous lowering profiles with their huge noses and pendulous lips! And besides, images of saints, even those painted in the most delicate pastels, though marginally tolerable in museums, simply weren't to be put on display in the everyday world. The Mary on the Half Shell decorating a front lawn, the pale plastic statue on a dashboard ("I don't care if it rains or freezes, 'long as I got my plastic Jesus..."), the Saint Christopher medal around a traveler's neck: revolting! And now here I am admiring a garish Virgin painted on a public wall. I guess that shows what Catholicism—even a relatively late conversion—can do to you.

On the whole, I do not regret my Protestant girlhood. With advancing age and accelerating physical debility, I have gotten out of the habit of regret. The alternative, I am afraid, would drive me mad, and I no longer wish to go mad, a state I endured with horror during my Protestant youth, not ever again. And anyway, the memories of Catholic girlhood I've read and listened to suggest that although I missed a great deal, most of it wasn't the sort of experience to be coveted. I've known woman after woman of my generation who still seethes about some elements of her religious upbringing: obtuse and even abusive nuns and priests who wielded Church doctrine along with yardsticks or birch switches to intimidate their young charges, inculcating superstition and self-hatred so poisonous that, even after decades at a safe distance, she still can't speak of those dreary years without a frisson of revulsion. In the long run, Congregationalism left me a little chilly, all the mystery scrubbed out of it by a vigorous and slightly vinegary reason, but hardly furious.

All the same, I do wish (and in this I may be more curious than rueful) that it had offered me the Blessed Virgin Mary. Or any feminine figure, for that matter. It may not have been altogether wholesome for a girl to grow up venerating women who leaped out of coffins and soared to the rafters to escape the stench of human flesh, like Saint Christina the Astonishing, or in response to compliments on their beauty rubbed pepper on their faces and lime on their hands, like Saint Rose of Lima. But another kind of soul-sickness, even more enervating in its way, arises in those deprived of any sense of identity with the divine. In Congregationalism I encountered a rather abstract but unequivocally masculine God and, of course, His Son, as well as a Holy Ghost, suitably attenuated and untainted by any association with Sophia. No saints, except the guys who composed the Christian Scriptures. And no holy representatives on earth, except maybe the minister, who was invariably—and without question—a man.

Prayer, within such a structure, was always to an Other, who could be counted on to judge but not always to understand, if you had your period, say, and needed the cramps to stop, or if you were crazy in love with your boyfriend and wanted more than life itself to go all the way and had no idea where you were going to find the strength to say no. This latter situation was especially troublesome, since in Congregationalism the loss of one's virginity was strictly prohibited without any notably spiritual point being put upon the matter. Because the King James Version, like others, reproduced the mistranslation *parthenos,* "virgin," for the Semitic term for a young unmarried woman, we referred to Jesus's mother as the Virgin Mary when we referred to her at all, which wasn't all that often, but no one ever suggested to me that I should preserve my virginity in order to emulate her chastity and obedience to God. No, mine was being "saved" for the husband I would inevitably have (though it wasn't until I discovered feminist theory twenty years later that I figured out why society thought it important enough to save). Not just her virginity, however, but also her motherhood would have provided a valuable model, in my struggles as a daughter and, not many years later, a mother myself.

Because I sensed a mysterious element here for which the utter virility of the Congregationalist Godhead failed to account, from early adolescence onward I coveted the saints (what little I could gather about them from books and films, having no Catholic friends), and especially Mary, whose multiplicity—maiden and mother intertwined—authenticated the personal mysteries I was destined to experience yet feared to endure without guidance. Her presence, if I could make it real in my life, could create spiritual space not for the encounter of God and man but for the bond between the Holy and me. Sometimes when alone I'd cross myself and murmur a Hail Mary, which I must have learned young from hearing the Rosary prayed as I twiddled the radio dial, and this habit persisted as I grew older. I did not pray to the Madonnas I studied in art class in college, but I contemplated their images—the severe dark skinny Byzantines, the luminous Italians—until they became a permanent part of my interior furnishings. Although I later named my daughter for my mother, I knew that the name Anne had belonged to Mary's mother, too. At last, I began to walk boldly into Catholic churches, forbidden me in my youth, staring—amused, awed, appalled—at painted statues got up in silk and stiff lace with browning bridal bouquets at their feet. In these ways, I suppose, I was preparing myself for the conversion I would eventually choose, whereby I claimed her for my own.

I don't know whether I'd have become a Roman Catholic had I remained in New England. But if I had, I feel certain that I would never have developed a devotion to Our Lady of Guadalupe. In fact, I'd probably never even have heard of her. In the area around Boston where I grew up, Catholic parishes tended to be identified ethnically. The Irish who went to St. Jude's would never have strayed into the Italian—or Portuguese or Polish or French Canadian—Sacred Heart across town. Even though Pope Pius XII designated Our Lady of Guadalupe "Empress of the Americas"—from Eagle, Alaska, to Tierra del Fuego, North, Central, and South—in 1945, only a church attended by Mexicans or Mexican Americans would likely be dedicated to her. And certainly none would be in Enon, Massachusetts. (Of the 106 such churches in the United States as of 1980,[1]

I doubt that any are in Massachusetts.) To find her, I really did have to move to the Southwest.

This matter of ethnicity has been a tangled one, right from the moment of her first apparition, on December 9, 1531, a decade or so after the Spanish conquistadores came to this continent, a long enough span for the native people who had greeted them as gods to figure out that they were human beings, and rapacious ones at that. In this bitter context, on Tepeyac Hill, at the edge of what is now Mexico City (a site already sacred to Tonantzin, snake woman and mother of gods[2]), an early convert to Catholicism, a Nahua named Juan Diego, was waylaid on his way to Mass by the sound of sublime music, perhaps birdsong. A young woman appeared and addressed him, using the affectionate diminutive "Juanito," little John. She was, she told him, the Virgin Mary, Mother of the True God, and she wanted a sanctuary to be built on that spot. He must take her message to the bishop of Mexico, Fray Juan de Zumárraga.

The bishop was polite enough, but skeptical, Juan Diego reported back to the Virgin, begging her to replace him with someone more eminent, and therefore more credible, than a peasant; but she wouldn't hear of it, and so he dutifully trudged back the next day to try again. This time Fray Zumárraga, still polite, asked for a sign, which the Lady promised to give Juan Diego the following day. Juan Diego's uncle fell ill, however, and Juan Diego stayed at home to care for him. On December 12, as he set out to fetch a priest to administer the last rites to his uncle, now dying, he was so chagrined to have missed his appointment that he tried to sneak around another way, but the Lady appeared nevertheless. Promising that his uncle would live (and indeed she appeared to the sick man and raised him from his deathbed), she sent Juan Diego up the barren hill to pick roses. These he bundled into his tilma, a cloak woven of fiber from the maguey plant, and carried to the bishop. When he unfolded the tilma, letting the roses tumble at Fray Zumárraga's feet, imprinted on it was an image, four feet eight inches high, of the

Lady whom Juan Diego and his uncle had seen. The astonished bishop did as he'd been asked.

Despite the fragility of cactus fiber, the tilma still exists—preserved after 1647 under glass, though it hung open to candle smoke and the lips and fingers of worshipers until then—in the Basilica of Our Lady of Guadalupe, second only to Rome as a center of pilgrimage in the Catholic world,[3] in northern Mexico City. The image it bears has been associated with miracles, beginning with the healing of Juan Diego's uncle and including the end of a flood in 1629 and of a plague in 1736.[4] In modern times, the artifact has received scientific scrutiny. Infrared photography, one biophysicist claims, reveals an original and quite simple image that is, in terms of the media used, "unexplainable as a human work,"[5] overlaid by later additions, perhaps to repair damage from the 1629 flood. Five ophthalmologists signed a certificate stating that, on examining the portrait's eyes with their instruments, they found themselves "looking into a human eye."[6] Even more astounding, those eyes have been found to contain the reflected images of Juan Diego, as he appears in a contemporary painting, together with his interpreter and an unidentified third person.[7]

Thanks perhaps to a persistent Protestant intractability, I have an uneasy relationship with the miraculous. In fact, the notion of a miracle as an act of God for my benefit, which seems to underlie the use of the word by the devout, embarrasses the hell out of me. When a woman tells me that she has just escaped death because, at the last moment, God deflected an onrushing car off the road and into the desert, I wonder how she accounts for all the collisions that do take place. Does God find those people unworthy of rescue? Or does God blink? Even though my joyous life is made possible by a miracle, George having survived metastatic melanoma for some years now, and even though the wailing infant in me petitions constantly *Dear God please please don't ever let him die and leave me*, I prefer not to look on his good health as a special favor from the Almighty lest I should, at remission's end, be forced to believe myself personally abandoned.

And so my mind scuttles away from flood and pestilence and La Guadalupana's mysterious eyes. With the political features of her manifestation, however, I can engage quite comfortably. In *indigenista* terms, her image and message clearly inform the issues of social justice that first drew me into Catholic practice and, against all odds, sustain me there. The figure, according to this interpretation, encodes the concepts necessary to effect the conversion of 8 million Indians in the seven years following the apparition.[8] (The desirability of becoming a Catholic is a moot point, I recognize, today as four centuries ago, but I won't get into it here. What's done is done.) To begin with, "Guadalupe" is probably a mistranslation, influenced by the shrine in Spain, of the name she spoke when she appeared to Juan Diego's uncle; she might more accurately be referred to as Our Lady of Tepeyac. Several Nahuatl alternatives have been suggested, the most widely accepted being "Coatlaxopeuh," that is, "she who crushed the serpent's head,"[9] which suggests the overpowering of the native gods by Christianity.

The icon itself reinforces this idea. It represents a woman with dark skin and hair (La Morenita, she is therefore sometimes called), her eyes downcast, in contrast to the straightforward gaze of Indian gods, and her hands raised before her in an Indian offertory gesture. She wears a rose-colored shift filigreed in gold, and over it a cloak of blue-green, a color reserved for the chief god Omecihuatl, or Ome-Teotl, scattered with gold stars auguring a new age. The black maternity band at her waist signifies someone yet to come, and below it, over her womb, may appear the powerful Mesoamerican cross to suggest just how mighty that Someone will be. The rays surrounding her form show her eclipsing the Sun Lord Tonatiuh; and the blackened crescent beneath her feet may be a phase of Venus, associated with Quetzalcoatl, the sacred Plumed Serpent. Hence the appropriateness of the name Coatlaxopeuh. She is borne by an intermediary "angel," the carrier of time and thus of a new era.[10]

Some of these signs seem hardly less fanciful than do miraculous remedies and mysterious ocular reflections, but that's not really their point. Their power lies in the suggestion that the Virgin appeared, long before the establishment of political boundaries in the "New World," to indigenous people whose old world had begun to crumble even before the Spanish invasion; she may thus signify both the "liberation and salvation" their prophets had predicted and the new spirit early Christian missionaries hoped to find here.[11] In this sense, she is a thoroughly American[12] saint, and her relegation by U.S. Catholics to Mexico and the Southwest, identifying her dark-skinned image with "an economically and socially unsuccessful and, hence, unacceptable ethnic group,"[13] probably does reflect bias against a minority woefully underrepresented among the clergy.

Ironically, however, this possibility strengthens her appeal for those of us, whether of Mexican heritage or not, who believe, as the Mexican American theologian Virgilio Elizondo puts it, that "the role of the powerless is to evangelize the powerful."[14] A reviewer of one of my books once took me to task for accepting the tenets of feminist and liberation theology merely on faith, as though one could not possibly, after long contemplation and appraisal, continue to affirm them. But God's preferential option for the poor —expressed at least as far back as Isaiah's cry for the protection of widows and fatherless children—rings true to my understanding of the Christian ethos. I must accept it, both on faith and on reflection, and act upon it if I am to carry out God's will. And in the tale of a dark-skinned peasant carrying to the conquistadores for their veneration the image of a dark-skinned Lady who promised her compassion to all humanity (even, I must suppose, the conquistadores) lies a model of the care I am, I believe, required to give.

*

She entered our urban, white, middle-class lives slowly. George and I had converted to Catholicism not for its saints but in spite of them; and not knowing quite what to do with them, we politely ignored them, the way you might some atavistic eccentricity in an otherwise sophisticated friend. This is rather hard to do if, every week of your life, you ask Blessed Mary Ever Virgin, all the angels and saints, and your brothers and sisters to pray for you to God. Clearly these holy figures were integral to spiritual health in a way we didn't quite fathom. Still don't, I might add, and probably never will. When I hear my elderly friends talk about Our Blessed Mother, I suspect you may have to be brought up Catholic to fully apprehend the role of an intercessor in devotional life. I still tend to talk to God directly, a habit fixed by the time I was thirteen, and probably nowhere near as courteously as Our Blessed Mother would do for me.

Since the need for an intercessor escapes me, when I do pray to the Virgin of Guadalupe, I pray to her directly too. It seemed natural, when our daughter left us to live in Africa, for George and me to light a candle in the lady chapel of our church after Mass each week and ask this mother figure to watch over Anne as her human parents could no longer do. Whenever someone we love is ill, we keep one of her candles burning constantly in our living room. I do not believe that such prayers "work" to effect a desired outcome (often referred to as a miracle)—a recently published, scientifically rigorous study suggests the contrary[15]—but they keep me attentive to the needs of others and remind me that that outcome will be what it will be.

Rather than a repository of prayer, Our Lady of Guadalupe primarily exhorts me to social action. In order to avoid being shut down by resentful neighbors, Casa María, the Catholic Worker house of hospitality in Tucson, was consecrated to her. The kitchen there is known as Our Lady of Guadalupe Chapel and Free Kitchen, and any tramp in the city can probably direct you to "Guadalupe's," identifiable by a brilliant painting of her on the wall beside the front door, where a sack lunch with soup is offered every day and Mass on Monday mornings. As George and I became increasingly involved in the community there, we began to think of her as the guardian of the thousand and more *pobrecitos* who lined up each day to be fed. At Guadalupe's, on Tucson's South Side, I learned to be among people-made-poor.[16] Until then, I considered myself one of the poorest people I knew. Probably I was. When my brother, then twelve, came to visit George and me and baby Anne, as he gazed out a side window of our cavernous apartment in downtown Waltham, Massachusetts, he said, "Nancy, is this a slum?" He'd been studying slums in seventh-grade social studies. It wasn't a slum (though it nearly qualified in cockroaches alone), but it was a far cry from the postcard village where he was growing up, as I had done twelve years before him. George and I had been married a good many years before we acknowledged that, living on the income of a couple of English teachers, we were never going to be the financial successes we'd been groomed to be. And it was a good many years after that before we recognized that we were nevertheless affluent beyond our wildest dreams. Our trip to Africa may have settled the matter once for all, but my serious education had begun among the tramps at Casa María.

While I was earning a Ph.D. in English and teaching freshman composition, I was being schooled in the radical democracy of God's Kindom. Contemplating the roots and repercussions of oppression, I was learning that no significant fundamental differences exist between me and every other member of humanity—none— but that discrepancies in access to power, and all the benefits that flow from it, are enormous. I have a little access. The man mumbling to demons outside the supermarket has none. The president of the United States has way more than is good for him—or the rest of the world, it seems. This insight, once achieved, both persists and insists. "Service to the poor" as a class becomes impossible. These are your sisters and brothers. You take care of them one by one. I wish I could say I had done my part to realize this egalitarian vision, but I haven't relinquished the material and social privileges I enjoy. Like the rich young man hearing Jesus's words, "If you would be perfect, go, sell what you possess and give to the poor, and you will have treasure in heaven; and come, follow me" (Matt. 19:21), I go away sorrowful. I do not doubt that if every human being followed this injunction, the world itself would become perfect. But if I, convinced of the virtue of voluntary poverty, have trouble lowering my standard of living (which is quite different from my quality of life) and recognizing that every person's worth is equivalent to my own, I must acknowledge the difficulty, even the impossibility, of converting six and a half billion people to lives of self-restraint and kindness. Difficulty and even impossibility are not excuses, however. I must work toward the kindom anyway, engaging in *tikkun olam*, the daily discipline of repairing the world, about which the Jewish *Mishnah* instructs that we are neither required to complete the task nor permitted to desist from it. That reality informs every act that fosters peace and social justice, *mitzvah* by *mitzvah*. It helps in this effort to have a model of all-inclusive care, as we do in La Guadalupana.

For my birthday one year George gave me a framed poster of her image. "What on earth will Mother say?" I wondered as we hung this icon on the bedroom wall. "Next thing you know, we'll be getting statues!" Sure enough. Above me as I write, in a niche formed by an old cooler duct, stands a porcelain Virgen (too white, but I was politically ignorant all those years ago when I bought her) surrounded by two garish plastic flowers made at a local senior center and the likenesses of the Dalai Lama, Dorothy Day, and the deep-blue Medicine Buddha. Now she is everywhere in our lives: on the painted tiles outside the front door; on a plaque enameled by Salvadoran refugees in Guatemala, where the hill she stands on is dotted with animals, including a fat armadillo; as a crude little figure carved out of wood, the rays around her formed out of yellow toothpicks. I even have her likeness hand-painted on a T-shirt by a Casa María worker, holding a soup ladle and a white Styrofoam cup. Nuestra Senora del Caldo, I call her. Our Lady of the Soup. Glimpses of these images each day as I move from task to task serve to remind me to be grateful for the gift of roses in midwinter and to pray for the protection of us all.

Now I wonder how I can locate the painter of that Lady and her resplendent serpent outside La Tiendita. I have this wide blank cream-colored wall to the right of my studio door . . .

A CALLING

Because these wings are no longer wings to fly
But merely vans to beat the air
The air which is now thoroughly small and dry
Smaller and dryer than the will
Teach us to care and not to care
Teach us to sit still.

T. S. ELIOT, "Ash Wednesday"

"I think," I said suddenly to my husband several years ago, "that I'm supposed to go to theological seminary." I did? If so, this was the first I'd heard of it. In Berkeley for a reading at a bookstore, we were stroll/rolling through the university campus on a mild November afternoon, and I suppose the proximity of the Graduate Theological Union had crossed my mind. Still, I'd been here any number of times without a stray thought for the GTU. Why on earth should this visit be any different?

"Supposed"? By whom? If I had been reared with the concept of vocation, I might interpret this unexpected revelation as a summons from God. In the upper-middle-class egalitarianism of the Congregational church to which my family belonged, however, the ministry was viewed as a profession much like any other. To be sure, the minister delivered a twenty-minute sermon on Sunday and visited the sick during the rest of the week instead of extracting teeth or drawing up wills, but otherwise he (and he was always a he) seemed little different from the rest of Enon's good citizens. His spiritual life lay, like everyone else's, strictly out of conversational bounds. An announcement that God wanted me to study Him (and He was always a He) would have been greeted with a certain embarrassed skepticism if not derision. Only hysterics heard the voice of God. Now I am a Catholic, part of an institution (made up of hysterics, some in my acquaintance would say) which has survived for centuries on the concept of religious vocation. I was drawn by the concept that not only did we need God but God needed us and that some people heard God calling them into relationship with the Holy. "If today you hear God's voice, harden not your hearts," admonishes the response to one of the psalms we recite during the Liturgy of the Word. But although I can now believe that others hear and heed God's call, to claim myself among them seems spiritually arrogant. Wanting some task carried out, God can do better than look to me. My own undertakings seem to reflect the will of God far less than they reveal my own willfulness. Whatever I've thought I was "supposed" to do, I've probably been the one supposing.

For the past several years, I have been swallowed up by the soul sickness known by the desert fathers as "accidie": the failure to respond to and act on a sense of divine purpose. "Sloth," we call it nowadays, and I will use the words interchangeably with the understanding that "sloth," in this context, signifies neither a hairy, slow-moving nocturnal beast nor mere lack of ambition but spiritual torpor seeping out of a miasma of distress and despair.

I am as accomplished at the seven deadly sins as most people, I'm sure, at some sins better than at others. Lust has pretty well left me, although not before adultery had wounded my husband, my other partners, and myself. Although I eat and drink more than I need and enjoy many material possessions, gluttony and greed have never driven me. I envy the accomplishments and sometimes the wealth of others but don't want to deprive them of their satisfaction;

I simply want to be satisfied too! I often seethe at circumstances but seldom at people. I slip into undeserved self-congratulation at the least provocation. With some success, I seek to practice their opposing virtues, to be chaste, moderate, generous, meek, charitable, and humble. By tradition, pride is the deadliest sin, but I suspect that this position may be occupied by different sins depending upon the person. For me, at this point the seventh sin—sloth—outranks the others, and its countervailing virtue, diligence, eludes me.

"I am no longer ert," as Prince Zorn laments in James Thurber's magical tale *The 13 Clocks*, "for I have lost my ertia." I can hardly work. Having published eight books, if I have another in me, I don't know what. I slump in front of my computer, playing solitaire, or fiddling with the software until I break and then have to fix it, or even merely staring at the screen. My mind oozes through ideas like a slug in an especially unkempt garden. Over and over I chastise myself for my dolor and lumpishness.

"Come on, Nancy," I caught myself scolding one day, "pull out of this paralysis and get to work." Then I had to think again, because I am in fact paralyzed, irreversibly and against my will, by multiple sclerosis. For about the first fifteen years after being diagnosed in 1972 with this chronic incurable degenerative disease of the central nervous system, I assumed that I would go on living the way my friends and colleagues were living, just with more effort. In this frame of mind, I reared my children, finished my Ph.D., taught university writing courses, wrote and published poems and essays.

Then I fell on my head. More than once. I gave up teaching. I sold my car. I sat down in a wheelchair for good. Even as I increased my efforts, my body was carrying me further and further away from the life I had intended to live. The truism designed to buck me up— you can do anything you want if you just try hard enough—turned out to be pure and rather cruel codswallop, suggesting as it does that if you fall short of a goal, you have only yourself to blame. After years of losing one competence after another, I can now do virtually nothing for myself except brush my teeth, and long experience has taught me that I will lose that ability as well. From the beginning I figured that life with MS was going to be hard. I never knew it would be this hard. Perhaps after more than a quarter of a century, the disease has worn me past the point of productivity by making the physical act of writing overwhelmingly arduous. My intellectual inertia might well have grown out of my physical immobility, leaving me paralyzed in more ways than one. In the face of my limitations, my spirit sags.

I speak, in conventional terms, of my "body" and my "spirit," as though the two were separate entities, even though from a biochemical perspective they probably are not. They certainly feel not just different but, at least in my case, alien to each other. I suppose what makes us human is precisely this illusion of divergence between material and spiritual being. Certainly when my cat tromps on my keyboard with all his twenty-six toes, he does so mindlessly, perfectly free from self-awareness (though I'm not so sure about self-satisfaction) in a way I can never be. My "I" feels trapped in a structure that I once imagined fondly as a house but that has metamorphosed under the baneful influence of MS into a prison. The inmate is intact, although because weakness renders speech and writing increasingly difficult, she must struggle to communicate the fact to the outside world. Immurement feels like a distinct and horrific possibility.

As I slouch here in my wheelchair, gasping with the terror of being buried alive, questions batter my brain. Who in the world benefits from my idleness, no matter how reluctant? Why am I still here? What on earth am I *for*? Beyond giving others the opportunity to practice the works of mercy at my expense, can I be said to serve any function at all? And if not, am I still fully human? In a society that conflates worth with productivity, can I learn to define humanness in other than utilitarian terms? "Do you think you're going to change the world?" a newspaper reporter once asked about my activism. "Well," I responded, "at least I'm not making it any worse." Is that enough?

That day in Berkeley, theological study may simply have seemed to offer the structure and purpose I want back in my life, and I may have implicated God in my urge only because the -logy my mind lit upon chanced to be theo- rather than anthropo- or psycho-. I've continued to be drawn to it. But I won't be going to theological seminary, even though I'm sure a year or two there would provide me both much-needed discipline and spiritual delight. Nor will I be doing much of anything else. My doing days are done.

And so I hunker, sullen and ashamed, in this slough. Something more than physical paralysis is at work here, something fiercer than MS daunts me: a loss of nerve beyond the neurological. Accidie appears to be as much a part of my reality as MS. No amount of resolve will rescue me. Nor can I "vanquish" either of them. This is not a war. This is a life, my life, and I have to work out how to live it meaningfully. If God does call me (and I must not discount such a possibility just because I seem a little hard of hearing), my response, whatever it might be, must take into account my paralysis of both body and will.

The doubt and dither I work myself into when I try to discern the way I ought to live and work arises from my childhood perception of God as Other, who might speak to me but probably would not, and indeed never did, strain though I might to hear His voice telling me exactly what He wanted me to do, when, and how often, so that I could become the good girl I was commanded to be. Such a view of the Holy as a vigilant alien being, the Big Boss, alternately instructive and punitive but always perfectionist, drew me deeply into the guilt and despair that characterized much of my life. My chosen Catholicism, I'm told, has done the same for countless others; but its emphasis on Incarnation brought me, entering as an adult, a fresh perception of the Good News (though not one the

Catholic Church would necessarily approve): that we bear God into the world, in all God's complexity, and so God is always with(in) us, to be welcomed time and again.

The Joseph of the Jesus narrative manifests the kind of awareness I have in mind. On the face of it, whoever put two and two together (so to speak) and figured out paternity did humankind an ambiguous favor. From that point on the male of the species could be obliged to assist in the support and rearing of his offspring, true, but he could also repudiate any child he even suspected of not being "his," thereby sparing himself no end of expense, not to mention the ignominy of having a woman, whose word was only as good as she was, put one over on him.

Not surprising, then, that Joseph—the product of a society as patriarchal as any ever contrived—should consider setting aside his intended when he learned she was pregnant. Why should he go to the trouble of rearing another man's child? In Matthew's Gospel he requires a miraculous, mystical experience to persuade him otherwise: a dream reassuring him that the child, though not his, belongs to no other man either. More miraculous to me is that an ordinary man could transcend social strictures in this way, welcoming a new life into his home for its own sake, not for his.

People do perform such gratuitous gestures. My own husband once offered to marry me under similar circumstances, and I have no doubt that he'd have been as faithful as Joseph in rearing an infinitely less gloriously fathered child, just as he was to the various others who have come our way.

One of these, an Athabaskan teenager, whom George met while teaching at a school for emotionally disturbed boys, and who became our foster son, sired our first two grandsons. These, in turn, have produced our four great-granddaughters, each with a different mother, none of them conceived or born in wedlock. Firm believers in two-parent families based on parental commitment to each other and to their offspring, we have nevertheless tried to make each one welcome in her turn, although only one has remained an active presence in our lives. Shortly after the first of them was born, I laughingly referred to my mother as a great-great-grandmother, and she visibly stiffened: "Oh no I'm not!" Even though I knew she had never accepted Ron as one of our children, had never welcomed his sons, I was taken aback by her vehemence. One would have thought I had called into question her own impeccable lineage by connecting her, however metaphorically, to this unfortunate product of the mindless coupling of a pair of fifteen-year-olds, who would likely become the mother of another such "surprise" in her turn. I felt sad that belief in blood and caste can still, two millennia after Joseph's tenderness toward what must have seemed a cuckoo's chick, so constrict the human heart as to exclude any child perceived to have sprung from the dreaded and despised "other."

What Joseph seems to have understood, when you strip away the fetters of custom and superstition overlaid upon the story to enhance its magical appeal, is that every infant bears the Holy into the world and must therefore be nurtured as one's own. Much is made of Mary's grace in accepting her lot as "an unwed teenage mother," as one slogan puts it, and we are admonished to model ourselves upon her trust in and compliance with God's instructions. But too often Joseph stands in the shadows of the stable, behind the crèche, his presence obscured by the bedazzled mother and the awestruck shepherds and the kings with their armloads of goodies, his role in the drama all but forgotten.

But Joseph's act reflects the very heart of the Gospel message: that we are to receive God in our midst at every moment through every creature. Imagine the transformation of the world if, like Joseph, we stopped distinguishing between our "own" children and those of the "other" and instead received all children as signs that God is with us. No longer could we drop bombs on Afghanistan or Iraq or anywhere else, because God would be pulverized many times over. We could not place an embargo on trade with countries like Cuba, lest God starve and sicken without food and medicine. We'd have to curb our use of fossil fuels or else God would scorch under the thinning ozone layer and smother in the polluted air. With faith and vision, we really could make these and other changes. They are not beyond our human capabilities. They are matters of choice. Whether we will choose or not is another matter. But we could.

When we choose an action, then, we must do so in good faith, attentive not to a set of regulations issued from on high but to our own best inclinations, which both arise from and attest to God's presence here, now, alive in us as in all creation. On the surface, a theology without a Watcher, separate and severe, might seem to invite moral laxity, but my experience suggests otherwise. Quite young children—even my dogs—can learn to behave well as long as a figure of authority is nearby to remind them what they may or may not do. The difference between them lies in the child's growing capacity to elect good behavior, not out of fear of retribution, hope of reward, or desire to please, but for goodness' sake. What God means us to do, as God's children, is not so much to perform this or that specific duty as to give our acts moral weight and take responsibility for them. Instead of relying on threats of perdition to whip us into right action, we are to heed the "ayenbite of inwyt," to use another medieval term: the remorse of conscience that develops and dwells within us.

Action itself is the commonly recommended remedy for accidie. "Get off your dead duff," my mother would admonish if she caught me moping about. She certainly wouldn't have recognized my condition as one of the deadly sins, and depression (which partially reflects the characteristics of accidie) wasn't readily diagnosed in children in the 1950s. She had the right instinct, nevertheless. The fifth-century monk John Cassian, following long-standing eremitical practice, prescribes work as the antidote to sloth's slow poison even if, like the hermit Paul, living too far from a market to peddle your baskets, you simply set fire to them once a year and start weaving new ones. The devil might or might not make work for my idle hands, but Mother wasn't taking any chances. I got busy, and I stayed busy.

It hadn't occurred to me until I began exploring the subject, however, that accidie might comprise busyness as well as shiftlessness, eroding the spirit even more insidiously because it masks its own vacuity. Thomas Aquinas notes that the "wandering of the mind after unlawful things" ascribed to sloth by the sainted pope Gregory I, "if it reside in the mind itself that is desirous of rushing after various things without rhyme or reason, is called 'uneasiness of the mind,' but if it pertains to the imaginative power, it is called 'curiosity'; if it affect the speech it is called 'loquacity'; and in so far as it affects a body that changes place, it is called 'restlessness of the body,' when, to wit, a man shows the unsteadiness of his mind, by the inordinate movements of members of his body; while if it causes the body to move from one place to another, it is called 'instability'; or 'instability' may denote changeableness of purpose."[1]

I've entertained these "daughters" of sloth, as Gregory calls them,[2] ever since Mother routed me from my easy chair and sent me hurtling through high school and college and graduate school, through marriage, motherhood, teaching, and on into writing. Only when I fetched up, breathless, here at my desk did I begin to think that my incessant actions might lead to some other end than simply getting through my life with as much dignity and satisfaction as I could. They might distract me from the fruitful attentiveness through which a person achieves balance and peace.

"I spend so much time planning all the things I have to do that I hardly pay attention to what's going on right now," my sister Sally said to me a couple of years ago, voicing a complaint that echoes throughout the lives of most of the people I know. Instead of falling naturally into what the contemporary Vietnamese Buddhist monk Thich Nhat Hanh calls "mindfulness," the mind behaves like a small furry animal scrabbling around the inside of the skull. The sillier the worries, the better it seems to like them. My own form of distraction tends toward planning what I am going to wear the following day (week, month, depending on how caught up I am in future events). If Sally meditated, her mind would certainly not wander off toward her wardrobe. I am the frivolous sister. But each of us in her own way loses focus.

I'm not saying that I have been too distracted to do good works along the way. At least from the time I became a Girl Scout leader at fifteen, I had a sense of social responsibility, although my activism didn't begin in earnest until a decade later. I have diligently performed the works of mercy myself, both corporal and spiritual. Even today I use up my limited energy hurrying from board meeting to reading engagement to worship service to demonstration, all worthy pursuits. I am hardly a fritterer. Rather, I am confessing that I have too often rushed around heedlessly, exploiting my good works as a means of deflecting or at least deferring the arduous spiritual work of defining and then fulfilling the purpose of my crippled life.

I have been looking at my life wrong way round. I have always assumed the existence of a paradigmatic "good" life, and believed I had the responsibility of aligning my own with it as closely as possible. To the extent that my life deviated from the model, I had failed and would have to work harder. If self-flagellation were still in vogue, a cat-o'-nine-tails would by now have grown into the flesh of my palm, so assiduously (and ineffectually) have I whipped my life into shape. Some shape: baggy and flaccid as an old rubber boot.

No matter how enfeebled my body has become, no matter how many physical limitations I have had to accommodate, I have never lived spiritually as though I have MS. I have lived as though I were "supposed" to compensate for having MS in order to fulfill the same duties as everybody else. When I could not, I have been angry at myself and ashamed at my shortcomings. I have not allowed myself to acknowledge that because my disease differentiates me in essential ways from the people I most admire, my duties may differ as well. No Peace Corps for me. No teaching poor children in East L.A. Not even any sandwich making at the local soup kitchen. I *feel* useless because I *am* useless. As long as I take this utilitarian view of my role in the world, I can only feel superfluous and burdensome. But alternatives to such a limited view must exist. During my years of Catholic praxis, I've gradually become familiar with the concept of "discernment." At first, I didn't pay it much attention, since I always heard it used in connection with religious vocation, and I never for a moment considered becoming a nun. But of course it has a perfectly secular meaning too—"the act or process of exhibiting keen insight and good judgment"[3]—and a spiritual one as well: "The aim of discernment is to enhance one's participation in the work of God, for the glory of God and the healing of the world."[4]

Recognizing the necessity for discernment, I have begun a couple of practices to slow my frantic pace. Every week at our nearby Episcopal church, a group of us sing the music of Taizé, an ecumenical community in southern France well known for its chants. I have also started the process of becoming an oblate at the Tucson monastery of the Benedictine Sisters of Perpetual Adoration, one of the "women and men, married or single, who, in their own way of life, with their ordinary family and social duties, find support and ongoing growth in holiness through spiritual association with a particular monastic community."[5] Through these, I want to learn to follow the holy injunction *be still*. Then maybe I can find out what I'm for.

We speak of "purposeful activity," after all. Why shouldn't there be such a state as "purposeful passivity"? Not the alternating lethargy and frenzy of the "noonday demon," as John Cassian calls accidie, but a deliberate quieting of the heart and opening of the spirit to the sacred in every moment, to the steady whisper (whose?) calling for attention: "Now! Now! Now!" Heard once, it will be easier to perceive the next time, and the next. Spiritual growth is not guaranteed by performing prescribed tasks or observing particular rules or rituals. Indeed, too rigorous an adherence to these can distract and dismay. The route to spiritual life lies in learning to listen. Perhaps I will sometimes be able to communicate what I have learned. Perhaps I will even write again now and then. With time and discipline, I will resign myself to my reality: I will do nothing easily. I will do most things not at all. I will learn to say, with the poet Theodore Roethke, "Being, not doing, is my first joy." I will hear God.

PART II

FAITH MATTERS: MEDITATIONS ON GOD, SIN, AND ABUNDANCE

POOR GOD

In these times we have to help God be God.

ETTY HILLESUM,
An Interrupted Life

I am fed up with feeling sorry for God. "Poor God," I sigh in response to one horrific headline after another, "the things they are doing in your name." The world is being battered senseless by bad news. God will love you on condition that you believe that Jesus will personally save you from the inconceivable horrors God has cooked up for everyone else. God will love you if you submit totally to God and use whatever means you can to expand the territory in which everybody else does so too. God will love you unless you permit the aforementioned expansionists to encroach upon the territory where you worship God. God will love you as long as you fight to the death to protect the land God gave you three thousand years ago, no matter who else lays claim to the same area and how many of them you have to kill in performing this sacred duty. All these messages reveal a great deal about human nature—the guilt, the fear, the territoriality, the arrogance—but virtually nothing about the Creator.

Recently, I've come to recognize that inward rue and apology are not good enough responses to the very public and often violent appropriation of God's name and God's will to justify such outrageous beliefs and behaviors. Although I have never quite overcome my embarrassment at speaking of these matters, repressed as reli-

51

gious utterance was first by my family and then by my protracted and thoroughly secular academic career, I now view my reticence as mere self-protection. Even though more than four out of five adults (84 percent) of people in the United States pray during a typical week, according to one study,[1] religion has taken on an unsavory character for many, appearing to have fallen into the hands of dirty old men or to have been co-opted by simpleminded little boys brandishing at some "evil" opponent a holy book in one hand and a weapon in the other. Who wants to engage in practices at the risk of being taken by the world for a pervert, a terrorist, a superstitious simpleton, or an outright nutter? I don't want to be taken for one of "them"—the ones who boast of possessing God's exclusive affection and consign to perdition all whose beliefs differ from theirs. I'd rather think like the Buddha, who says in the Majjhima Nikaya: "Apart from consciousness no absolute truths exist. False reasoning declares one view to be true and another view wrong. It is delight in their dearly held opinions that makes them assert that anyone who disagrees is bound to come to a bad end. But no true seeker becomes embroiled in all this. Pass by peacefully and go a stainless way, free from theories, lusts, and dogmas."

I know God. I do not mean that I have a special intimacy with God, either direct or mediated by some human or divine representative. I know God in the way that anyone is aware of the reality in which she is embedded. And what I know differs so radically from the views commonly taken as "religious" nowadays that I feel compelled to speak out. By so doing, I intend to redeem God from the ones who hold the Holy One captive in their own system of belief. Failing to perceive that Yahweh, Shekhinah, Allah, the Buddha, Krishna, Olorun, Áwonawilona, and countless other focuses of worship manifest Holiness, no one of them more than any other since Holiness cannot exceed itself, God's captors each believe they've laid hands on the "true" God, as though God could be anything but True. They snap and snarl and tear at one another's flesh like curs while God watches, weeps, and (I'll have to return to this point again and again) embraces them all.

The compulsion I feel is not imposed by God. God does not want me to speak out in defense of the Holy, any more than God wants one political candidate or another to be president of the United States or the United States to dominate the world, whether economically, politically, or religiously. God does not want. Period. That's not who or how God is. The need to reduce God to a person having mental states with which we are familiar—desire, anger, retribution (but seldom, alas, a sense of humor)—does God little service and ourselves even less. We would do better to stand before God in silence, allowing the Holy to open to us without our definition or direction. Only God can say what God is. We can only allow ourselves to be taught.

Sometimes the lessons can be a little rough. A few years ago, not for the first time, I fell flat on my face. Literally. In my life, multiple sclerosis serves to translate metaphor back into materiality, as I bear ample scars to attest. This time, purple stained my swollen left eye and jaw; the crowns on my two front teeth, put in place after an earlier fall, chipped; my lips puffed out in a parody of a sexual pout; and inside the lower lip, four sutures held together the raggedly bitten flesh. As the swelling pressed both inward and outward, I floundered in a fog of painkillers, hating them but grateful for the periods of respite they afforded. Just then I also fell flat on my face figuratively, yet another grant application turned down, and no anodyne could dull the stab of despair this sort of rejection always brings. Body and soul united in one long moan.

I can't count the number of times I've been told, often by strangers as they observe my crippled form, "God never sends us more than we can handle." I know that they mean to comfort me for what they assume, quite wrongly, to be a wretched fate, and so I grit my teeth and smile—but weakly. I despise pious clichés, not merely because they falsify experience (most of us face, from time to time, more than we can handle) but because they distance and distort the Holy. "God" doesn't "send" the events of our lives, for good or ill. What happens, happens.

On rainy days, which come seldom enough in the desert, my elderly white cat used to stare out the back door, then turn his green gaze on me and open his pink maw. "Mwrk!" he would say in a voice ridiculously ill-suited to his bulk.

"Don't look at me," I told him every time. "I didn't do it. It's not my fault." He never believed me. Why should he? I caused the kitty kibble to materialize in his bowl. Mine was the warmth against which he pressed, rumbling sonorously, on winter nights. With me around, doors opened and closed at his petition and dreadful shouts issued forth whenever he chased the black cat, equally elderly and a quarter his size. And every so often, despised water descended from the sky, flooding the hollows under the privet where he preferred to lie before an owl swooped from nowhere one night and carried him away.

Winchester was entitled to his magical sense of my powers. His brain was the size of an immature brussels sprout at best and, since he was FIV+, shrinking. In infancy, human creatures, though differently endowed, make similar conjectures. All of us go through a stage of belief in the Almighty Parent before whom we are powerless, who dispenses and withholds at will, who knows our every thought and action even when out of view and judges them, often severely. But we can go through it into a spiritual adulthood in which we recognize that God, though infinitely mysterious, is no magician, is not indeed an entity at all but rather an eternal unfolding in which all creation—even Winchester, even I—have our parts and bear our responsibilities.

No Force hurled me from my wheelchair facedown on a tiled floor. Heedlessly, I left my wheelchair turned on and struck the joystick with my forearm, whipping around with such momentum that

I pitched out. In future, I would be wise to attend to the little red button more closely. Nor did any Intelligence poison the minds of a panel of judges against my work. I have perhaps mistaken my own merits, or the judges have, but God surely has not.

What happens, happens. The Anglo-Saxons had a word for this observation, *wyrd,* which they used in ways that resemble our use of "fate" or "divine will." Perhaps because my lineage can be traced to the speakers of that flinty tongue, I am drawn to the tone of resignation in the word, the sense—born perhaps of a severe climate with a short growing season when there were few remedies against exposure, starvation, and illness—that events simply occurred, unwilled, uncontrolled. This did not lead to defeatism, since I am here to affirm that the race survived, but to a kind of immersion in and acquiescence to whatever life brought next.

If there's anything the modern mind cannot bear, it's the suspicion that no one is in charge. Individuals want to control their own destinies, and they expect assistance in the venture from a variety of social institutions. If a smooth course gets disrupted, someone can always be found to blame: the negligent parent, the inept schoolteacher, the corrupt cop, the sleazy manufacturer, the greedy lawyer, the power-hungry politician. Most would not lump God in with this unsavory assembly, but in attributing life's accidents to Him, unconsciously they make of God a similarly remote and even inimical Other (to whom they invariably refer with the masculine pronoun) just for the reassurance that Somebody is in control. After reading an early draft of this essay, a friend protested: "You explain how our expectations of God, and our tendency to blame God, rest on a false image of God as Parent, and often as negligent parent. I find it hard not to blame God. I guess I don't try not to. I get the impression that I'm not supposed to have expectations of God. Please fill me in here, because I have Great Big Expectations of God, and as usual, God is not measuring up."

I know just how she feels! But no, I don't have expectations of

God. Maybe I'm just perpetuating my childhood habit of refusing to hope for whatever I wanted for Christmas so as not to endure the inevitable deluge of disappointment when I didn't get it (and I usually didn't). Nowadays, though, I don't ask for anything for Christmas, because I don't need anything (never mind what I might want). My sense of God has evolved over time, as has God Godself, and I am better at embracing chaos, which has, physicists have discovered, its own weird elegance, and to admit that no Supreme Being stands outside creation taking charge of the events that befall us in the comforting way the vestigial infant in each of us would like to think. God is the whole: the fall, the pain, the healing, the new fall …We are never left alone to face the tests an Almighty Examiner chooses to set for us. We, like the rest of creation, are in God, of God, and God is unfailingly present as Whatever Happens Next.

For many of us, the idea of God as a verb—a process, specifically an unfoldment, without origin, without end, without site or stint or cease—seems too vast and cold to provide the sense of spiritual relationship we crave. We simply don't relate to processes. We may observe them, we may participate in them, but we don't talk to them person to person. We need a listening entity. We need God to sit still. I think of God in terms of rudimentary quantum mechanics: as a wave until collapsed into a particle by my focus. In this state, God can be imagined as a static Being who can be addressed. When I look away, God reverts to waviness and flows on. The particulate form provides me the means to speak both to and about the Holy.

"I love your image of God as 'wave' and God as 'verb,' " wrote my friend, a Catholic fallen away and now uncertainly tottering back. "I am scrambling to find more association because this God sounds detached to me. And silent. Does 'wave' God or 'verb' God love me? Talk to me? How does this God relate to my joy, to my serving in God's name? Does 'wave' God or 'verb' God move purposely? Feel?

How does this God relate to my/your suffering, to your MS? Does God just look at me when I suffer, shrug, and think, 'Oh, well. Too bad.' Does God think?" I was struck dumb, not because I didn't understand her questions but because the dynamic God she refers to so transcends language and all my other human faculties that I didn't know what to say. Of the God I can net with words I can say: Yes, God loves me, welcomes my gratitude, rejoices with me, weeps with me, suffers with me. To God in this form I can pray.

Although I believe that perfect prayer should consist of praise for the All and meditation on the Mystery at its heart, my own prayer tends to lapse into petitions to a sort of Parent: "please, please, please." I tend to pray hastily, often in a panic, or by rote. I'm most apt to ask for trivialities, like money, or impossibilities, like being cured of my multiple sclerosis. I don't believe in divine intervention. I believe in miracles, but only as random inexplicable events. I know that God doesn't hand out treats in return for my good behavior, just as I feed biscuits to my Labrador retriever when he sits on command; nor does God chastise me for my sins. I am not the object of the Almighty's operant conditioning. Nevertheless, a low mutter—even a whine—of petition accompanies me throughout my days.

I am shamed by the baseness of my spiritual life, but I also recognize petitionary prayer as a habit developed out of that magical childhood thinking I mentioned earlier. I want my own way. I want God to give it to me. Right now. The fact that we "outgrow" childhood doesn't mean that we shed it altogether; every phase of our selves dwells in us and informs subsequent development. Not surprising, then, that old elements emerge and reemerge, often without any apparent reason, like the dark heads of seals erupting through the ocean surface. The challenge is to identify and acknowledge them without permitting them to cramp mature experience. Maybe one day I'll achieve the range Dorothy Day captures in noting that all prayers, no matter what the words, are really one of five prayers: Thank you; Lord, have mercy; God damn it!; Help!; and Wow!

Some people get stuck. Some people make a religion out of their stuckness. In it lies the basis of fundamentalism, I think. The deity is represented psychically as a forbidding Father who looms out of the primal scene to pronounce a long list of commandments and an even longer one of prohibitions on pain not merely of death but of infinite torment, an orientation corresponding to the most elementary stage of moral development. He has revealed these principles once for all in sacred writings or oral tradition to a chosen and enlightened segment of humanity, often requiring that His followers proselytize nonbelievers and, in some practices, exterminate whoever refuses to convert. Both speculation and diversity are anathema.

The payoff for adopting the posture of a child who is sure to perform all manner of bad behavior unless obedient to God's strict tutelage? Absolute assurance of God's protection of and preference for the self (and, by extension, those who share the self's beliefs and practices) and, for obeying the rules, the reward of a lifetime: heaven. When Terry Gross, host of NPR's *Fresh Air*, asked Tim La-Haye, coauthor of the wildly successful Left Behind series of novels, whether he believed that he would go to heaven, he replied without a nanosecond's hesitation that he was confident of it but that she, a Jew, would not. Many of us would have to scrutinize our consciences, and in the unlikely event that we found nothing blameworthy there, we might still conclude that God will have to decree our ultimate destination when the time comes. But once a fundamentalist subscribes to a set of divine precepts, the way to eternal bliss is clear and unquestionable.

I do not doubt that such a belief system consoles its adherents; and I would happily leave them to their comfort—in this harsh world where one may fall on one's face at any moment, who could begrudge it?—if only they would leave me to mine. But because a fundamentalist system is rooted in teachings believed to be absolute and inerrant, the spiritual flexibility I enjoy can only be condemned as heterodoxy and sacrilege. A system so rigid and fearful walls God up with His believers in a hermetically sealed box, a big one, often crowned with a dome or a steeple, or a little one in which God Himself has scribbled His instructions. Probably I cannot persuade its adherents to open their souls and embrace the Whole in which they live. No word can breach that barrier. All I can do is reveal what I know.

I often cast my meditations in terms of Jesus's teachings because my entire life has been steeped in them, not because I consider them uniquely apt. They echo and are echoed in utterances about sacred matters throughout history. I do not believe that "Whoever believes in him will not be condemned, but whoever does not believe has already been condemned, because he has not believed in the name of the only Son of God" (John 3:18). You do not have to believe in Jesus Christ in order to lead a holy life. I do not know why anybody would tell you that you did, unless to scare you into being good by threatening you with untold horrors in the afterlife, where wickedness must be punished since it is so seldom on this side of the grave. I'm not persuaded that there is an afterlife, not in the sense most people conceive it, but if there is, I doubt that it will be given over to your chastisement. No, I'm afraid you'll have to be good on your own, without threats or bribes, although the Jesus of the Gospels provides some helpful instructions.

You don't even have to believe in God in order to be good. That is, God will enter the world through you whether or not you think that God exists. Lately, I've begun to wonder whether the world and all its denizens might be more likely to survive if fewer people believed in what they call "God" (or "Allah" or what have you), since the deity they construct and worship is so often dangerously cruel, exclusive, and demanding. This one (and many faiths insist that "He" is one, even though they obviously have no idea what oneness is), inviting division and intolerance, can hardly be called "holy."

In short, millions of self-identified religious people just don't "get" God. In this regard, Eastern teachers better communicate the quiet receptivity true holiness requires. According to the eighth-century Chinese monk Pai-chang, "Since there has been enlightenment in the past, there must also be enlightenment in the present. If you can attain now and forever the single moment of present awareness, and this one moment of awareness is not governed by anything at all, whether existent or nonexistent, then from the past and the present the Buddha is just human, and humans are just Buddhas."[2] Moreover, as Thich Nhat Hanh makes clear, we are essential to the presence of the Holy among us: "When we say, 'I take refuge in the Buddha,' we should also understand that 'The Buddha takes refuge in me,' because without the second part the first part is not complete. The Buddha needs us for awakening, understanding, and love to be real things and not just concepts. They must be real things that have real effects on life. Whenever I say, 'I take refuge in the Buddha,' I hear 'the Buddha takes refuge in me.'"[3] Thought about in terms of such reciprocity, God cannot be a possessible entity, the property of some, the enemy of others. God comes to us all, bidden or unbidden, and we all serve as God's safe haven.

Even though I don't fret whether anyone else believes in God, I am happy that I do. Awareness that I am immersed in the Holy encourages me to attend to and appreciate every element I encounter. I do so more readily with some creatures, objects, and events than others, I confess; and I do so more happily with those I can admire than with those I must endure, admonish, or correct. With certain politicians I have so far failed altogether. Seriously, in God I know that all creation is interconnected and sacred and that I must live in it responsively and responsibly. I don't think that my belief confers meaning to myself or anything else. I'm pretty sure that the cosmos is meaning-less in any human sense of the word, without purpose or consequence. It is not *for*. It is. Yahweh, in Hebrew Scripture: I Am. What God offers is not significance for a chosen few but mystery for whoever chooses to perceive it, an inexhaustible arouser of devout astonishment.

GOD IN LOVE

*Those who attain perfect wisdom are forever inspired
by the conviction that the infinitely varied forms of this
world, in all their relativity, far from being a hindrance
and a dangerous distraction to the spiritual path, are really
a healing medicine. Why? Because by the very fact that
they are interdependent on each other and therefore have
no separate self, they express the mystery and the energy
of all-embracing love. Not just the illumined wise ones
but every single being in the interconnected world is
a dweller in the boundless infinity of love.*

PRAJNAPARMITA

Here's the gist of sin and salvation, gleaned from the second of more
than 10 million results of a Google search for the phrase "find Jesus":

Think about this . . . God, out of profound love for you—a vile
sinner who has transgressed His commandments—let His own
beautiful, dear Son be sacrificed for YOUR sins! Jesus wasn't a
sinner. He didn't sin one time. He didn't die for Himself. He
died for you. To save YOU. That's why He is called the Saviour.
Because He SAVES from hell! If you reject His sacrifice and
trod it underfoot it should not be too hard for you to understand
that the same God who sacrificed His beloved Son will expedi-
tiously cast your rebellious hind parts into hell and the lake of
fire. NOTHING unclean will ever enter God's heaven—and all

62

unregenerate people are unclean. I too was once dead in tres-
passes and sins, but one lovely day I turned my face to Jesus and
got washed in the blood. You can too—no matter what you've
done.[1]

These words appear on a Web site directed to "all King James 1611
Bible-believing Christian friends"[2] by a woman who identifies
herself only as Tracy. After spending too many minutes here, browsing through parts of the most virulent anti-Catholic diatribe I've
ever encountered, I decide to spare myself the other 10 million hits.
I think I've got enough to grapple with already: sacrifice, vileness,
hell, and a very peculiar and puzzling sort of ablution.

Our lives are the stories that we tell ourselves about ourselves.
Without this narrative capacity, we would simply experience random events, without apparent cause or significance, like the sudden
disintegration of the young mesquite tree in my backyard. Although
I wasn't present, I have a rough sense of the collapse, having to do
with a central crack and the ill-advised removal of a prop and a
microburst of hot desert wind. The mesquite has no idea what
happened. Trees require no explanations. But we human beings,
both saddled and blessed with consciousness, need to identify
events, interpolate them into the ongoing annals of our existence,
and interpret them in the light of all we know so far. "Reality" is
unquestionably even more chaotic than the jumble of windblown
branches outside my door would suggest. But, as T. S. Eliot's mysterious bird tells us in "Burnt Norton," "human kind cannot bear
very much reality." And so we select and organize as much information as we can from the data pelting us from every direction.

Because I didn't witness the original event, I might offer a different explanation for the wreckage of my tree from the one I've
just given. I might say, for example, that a mesquite-malevolent
force hurled a thunderbolt at the heart of my hapless tree, blow-
ing it apart. I might even say that the malevolence was directed to-

ward me, not my vegetation, that I deserved the loss of shade at the beginning of Tucson's punishing summer as retribution for some sin or another. Heaven knows I have enough of them, all the seven deadlies and a few more besides. The relative plausibility of these alternative theories doesn't concern me here. The point is that we have considerable imaginative latitude in accounting for the mysterious elements in our lives.

In that case, why do we tell ourselves stories as horrific as the one above—and many, many people do portray their lives in terms this lurid or even worse. What kind of a father makes of his son a blood sacrifice as atonement? (True, Abraham was on the brink of doing so to Isaac, but Abraham was a doddering old man who heard voices, not a deity.) What kind of a God would permit such an act for His own satisfaction? How does a demand for death reflect profound love and why would the bearer of such love consign any part of the beloved's anatomy to a lake of fire? Why do we assume ourselves to be so loathsome as to deserve such treatment? By what means does a bath of blood lead, even symbolically, to purification? The God at the center of this plot, angry and abusive, arises out of terror, as though He were an angry father swaggering about and swinging his belt, ready to give us what-for (for our own good, of course). Who would boast of such beliefs and try to get others to share them, condemning anyone who refused? Who would comply?

When I try to imagine a believer who promulgates the creed that Jesus Christ died for my sins and only through him can I be saved from perpetual torment, then, I see a very small and very frightened child—just the person who least needs a tale mired in evildoing, singed by eternal flame, and soaked in blood. I want to take this bewildered child in my arms and whisper, "Don't be scared. You're just having a very bad dream. The evil creature you believe to be stalking you is not the devil but a bogeyman, and the lake of fire into which you fear you'll be thrown is just a mirage. No matter what you have done or what you believe, you are safe in God." Let us stop right here and tell the story another way, addressing at the out-set the child—ignorant and fragile—who lives in us all. Here's a lighthearted version e-mailed to me recently by my foster daughter, the mother of three:

> After creating heaven and earth, God created Adam and Eve. And the first thing he said was "DON'T!"
>
> "Don't what?" Adam replied.
>
> "Don't eat the forbidden fruit," God said.
>
> "Forbidden fruit? We have forbidden fruit? Hey Eve, we have forbidden fruit!!!!!"
>
> "No way!"
>
> "Yes way!"
>
> "Do NOT eat the fruit!" said God.
>
> "Why not?"
>
> "Because I am your Father and I said so!" God replied, won-dering why He hadn't stopped creation after making the ele-phants. A few minutes later, God saw His children munching an apple and He was angry! "Didn't I tell you not to eat the fruit?" God asked.
>
> "Uh-huh," Adam replied.
>
> "Then why did you?" said the Father.
>
> "I don't know," said Eve.
>
> "She started it!" Adam said.
>
> "Did not!"
>
> "Did too!"
>
> "DID NOT!"
>
> Having had it with the two of them, God decreed their pun-ishment: Adam and Eve should have children of their own.

All of us feel certain that we once dwelled in a Garden of per-fect innocence, and that we would dwell there still if we hadn't fallen victim to our wayward desires, though we may express our fundamental grief at our expulsion from the Edenic environment of the womb in countless tropes. Those of us steeped in the literature and art of Western Europe inherit Adam and Eve and the wily serpent even if we profess no religion—and with them a dread of our natural depravity. Christianity, in particular, "demands, at the very least, the inevitable emergence of creatures capable of sin. Without a history of human sin, there is no Christ"[3] since, after all, atonement becomes superfluous in the absence of anything to atone *for*. But I think the story of Adam's "fall" deepens if we read it as a narrative in which disobedience is not wicked but necessary in order for us to mature morally. In this interpretation, God is less a forbidding father than an anxious parent, who knows that once Adam and Eve (and all of us through them) become fully cognizant, they will comprehend the hardships of their lives and their own mortality. And so God admonishes them as we do our own children: *Don't do that, or else...* Actions have consequences, sometimes very disagreeable ones, and we hope that our warnings will hold them back from the pain we wish to spare them. Like any loving parent, God doesn't lock the children up, however, but leaves them free to act on the advice—or not.

But look at the situation from Eve's, and then Adam's, point of view. Essentially, God is trying to keep them from growing up, the serpent suggests. There won't really be any consequences (don't we always hope this when we do something we oughtn't?). Eve knows better: "God said, 'You shall not eat of the fruit of the tree which is in the midst of the garden, neither shall you touch it, lest you die.'" But she eats anyway, and Adam does too, without protest. "Then the eyes of both were opened" (Gen. 2:7). Their innocence at an end, they embark on the journey toward moral development, one that each of us must take in turn, learning to choose, sometimes painfully, between good and ill.

Thus, the story of Eve and Adam recapitulates the exile of all of us from an undifferentiated and paradisial infancy and our emergence into the moral world. The capacity to distinguish good from evil may render us, as the serpent hisses, "like God"; but if so, the resemblance (and it is only a very limited resemblance) comes at a steep price. We can now evaluate our own actions. And in doing so, we often come up against a distressing reality: no matter how honorable our intentions, our thoughts and behaviors seem frequently to have unpleasant consequences. In short, we begin to experience ourselves as wrongdoers.

Out of the primitive developmental phase in which parental power is mystified and parental displeasure is dreaded grows the concept of "original sin," caused by the disobedience of our First Parents, handed down from one generation to the next, and atoned for by the death of Jesus. It has dogged Christianity—and indeed, for some denominations, provided its raison d'être—at least since Saint Paul wailed, "For I delight in the law of God, in my inmost self, but I see in my members another law at war with the law of my mind and making me captive to the law of sin which dwells in my members. Wretched man that I am! Who will deliver me from this body of death?" (Rom. 7:22–24). Just as Eve and Adam's first impulse after gaining awareness of good and evil is to cover their nakedness, Paul's words clearly suggest that the root of the problem lies in sex, since "member" may refer to a limb but more commonly means the penis. Most of humanity, not just Christians, have been impelled since time immemorial by the sexual anxiety that begins probably before we learn to speak. This in itself is neither good nor bad. It's just part of who we are. But to convert it into religion and erect whole legal structures upon it seems unpardonably naive. God expects us to know better.

"Sin" is a subtler concept than it appears at first glance. The concrete meaning in Hebrew and Greek is to miss the mark, as an arrow flies past a target, and this image captures the combination of good intention and errancy that characterizes most transgression.

Although it is not intrinsically evil, it can easily be misconstrued that way, depending as it does on an understanding of God's law, which requires constant reflection, since the law is not (though it may once have been) engraved in stone. Even the commandments that seem most universal may not apply to all people in the same way at all times. Certainly most of us agree that stealing is wrong yet would view the behavior of a drug-addicted burglar who breaks into a home and steals a family's Christmas presents as qualitatively unlike a father's theft of bread to feed his children and both of these as different from a CEO's embezzlement that bankrupts a company and throws hundreds of people out of work. The moral life is an arduous one, demanding that every situation be scrutinized on its own merit; even then, a decision may have multiple consequences, some beneficial and others harmful. The stolen bread might allay the children's pangs, but the grocer receives no compensation— and his children must eat, too. Consequences are seldom pure.

Some people, troubled by ambiguity, collapse the world into just two categories, "good" and "evil" (which too often means "everybody whose beliefs differ from my own"), and claim to know who or what belongs in each, a certitude that smacks of the sin of pride, of pretending to be "like God." The trouble with this view of morality lies in its inflexibility. Every group, defining its own beliefs and behaviors as good, righteous, even stamped with God's personal approval, has only the idea of an opposite with which to identify all who believe and behave differently. They share the vision of the Puritan Jonathan Edwards predicting for Judgment Day: "When the saints in glory, therefore, shall see the doleful state of the damned, how will this heighten their sense of the blessedness of their own state, so exceedingly different from it!"[4] It is a closed system in which everybody, regardless of creed or practice, thinks in the same way. When Muslim extremists point at America and scream, "You're the Great Satan and we have to blow you up," we shout back, "No, you're the Great Satan and we have to bomb your countries," for all the world like the fractious children who made God wish to have stopped with the elephants, only grown large and deadly. No one dares step outside the good/evil paradigm and invent some altogether different structure for human interaction. We could have helped to overturn any number of dictators if, instead of squandering billions of dollars on ordnance, we had bombarded their countries with butter, medications, and wireless devices; a healthy, well-fed, and well-informed populace is much less vulnerable to oppression. If battles there must be, they can fight their own.

To our peril throughout the ages, dualism has been humanity's most prevalent mode of constructing the world, however. Is it because we have two of everything? If we grew three hands or three feet, would we think outside the binary box? Fortunately, it is possible, without drastic evolutionary modification but with vigorous practice in discernment, to conceive the world otherwise: not in terms of dyads—good opposed to evil, right opposed to wrong, you opposed to me—but more realistically and fluidly. Those who can do so—and this includes not only Christians but practitioners of all faiths—make no judgments on God's behalf but pray for guidance in their own decisions and actions and then for mercy for all the times these fall short.

Any number of times when I've attended an Ash Wednesday service, the priest has observed, looking out across the overflowing chapel, that more people go to church on this day than on any other. Neither of the great festivals, Christmas and Easter, draw as many worshipers. Ash Wednesday marks the beginning of the second great penitential season in the liturgical year, and such high attendance attests to a fundamental human characteristic: our preoccupation with wrongdoing and atonement. Knowing ourselves to be sinners, we aren't satisfied simply to acknowledge our transgressions. We want to *do* something about them. People who envision God as a remote and fearsome judge may be motivated by the fear that they will be thrown into hell in punishment for breaking divine decrees too numerous to mention (there are more than six hundred such laws in the first five books of the Bible alone). Those of us for whom God is a beloved presence manifest in everyone we meet, because we believe that God grieves over our faults, seek to make amends to anyone we have injured. Regardless of impetus, believers welcome Lent as a period for contrition.

Over the centuries, in accord with the Pauline condemnation of the flesh and encouragement of its mortification, some expiatory acts took on extreme forms: sleeping on hard pallets; wearing itchy garments or even barbed wire next to the skin; beating oneself bloody with knotted thongs; starving to the verge of death and beyond. Some of these practices persist to this day, but many would now question how anyone can have a healthy relationship with God while in a daze of pain and deprivation. Nor does Scripture suggest that we ought to get ourselves into such a state. What we need in order to please God, the Psalmist sings, is not a holocaust but a willing spirit, a clean and contrite heart. To achieve these does require discipline, of course. I elect to abstain from meat on Fridays (and as many other days as practicable) during Lent, not as a means of self-castigation but as a reminder to reflect upon and rectify my shortcomings, but I wouldn't expect this practice to be meaningful for everyone. Our sins take many different forms; no doubt our penances will vary, too.

Since the thought of dying mystifies and appalls us more than any other, death has long been imagined as the ultimate punishment, meted out, in biblical terms, to our First Parents and through them to the whole of humanity: "through one person sin entered the world, and through sin, death, and thus death came to all," Paul asserts (Rom. 5:12), and Church teaching has emphasized this connection ever since. All the same, death seems an awfully steep price to pay for a bite or two of a sweet, stolen fig. Unless, in connecting the two, Paul means by "sin" something more than succumbing to the desire for forbidden fruit and by "death" something else than the exhalation that marks the flight of the spirit from its prison of flesh, but I'm not sure that he does. Paul can be dismayingly literal. Most of us think of sin (insofar as we think of it at all) as a kind of glorified rule-breaking. Like children, we want clear instructions and are made nervous by their absence. God, through Moses, laid down specific commandments, and as long as we follow these, we figure we can't go far wrong. A send-up of the need for regulation, "An Open Letter to Dr. Laura," has circulated on the Internet for several years, directed to a popular radio personality who had dubbed homosexuals a "biological error."

Dear Dr. Laura,

Thank you for doing so much to educate people regarding God's Law. I have learned a great deal from your show, and I try to share that knowledge with as many people as I can. When someone tries to defend the homosexual lifestyle, for example, I simply remind him that Leviticus 18:22 clearly states it to be an abomination. End of debate.

I do need some advice from you, however, regarding some of the specific laws and how to best follow them.

a) When I burn a bull on the altar as a sacrifice, I know it creates a pleasing odor for the Lord (Lev. 1:9). The problem is my neighbors. They claim the odor is not pleasing to them. Should I smite them?

b) I would like to sell my daughter into slavery, as sanctioned in Exodus 21:7. In this day and age, what do you think would be a fair price for her?

c) I know that I am allowed no contact with a woman while she is in her period of menstrual uncleanliness (Lev. 15:19–24). The problem is, how do I tell? I have tried asking, but most women take offense.

d) Lev. 25:44 states that I may indeed possess slaves, both male and female, provided they are purchased from neighboring nations. A friend of mine claims that this applies to Mexicans, but not Canadians. Can you clarify? Why can't I own Canadians?

e) I have a neighbor who insists on working on the Sabbath. Exodus 35:2 clearly states he should be put to death. Am I morally obligated to kill him myself?

f) A friend of mine feels that even though eating shellfish is an abomination (Lev. 11:10), it is a lesser abomination than homosexuality. I don't agree. Can you settle this?

g) Lev. 21:20 states that I may not approach the altar of God if I have a defect in my sight. I have to admit that I wear reading glasses. Does my vision have to be 20/20, or is there some wiggle room here?

h) Most of my male friends get their hair trimmed, including the hair around their temples, even though this is expressly forbidden by Lev. 19:27. How should they die?

i) I know from Lev. 11:6–8 that touching the skin of a dead pig makes me unclean, but may I still play football if I wear gloves?

j) My uncle has a farm. He violates Lev. 19:19 by planting two different crops in the same field, as does his wife by wearing garments made of two different kinds of thread (cotton/polyester blend). He also tends to curse and blaspheme a lot. Is it really necessary that we go to all the trouble of getting the whole town together to stone them? (Lev. 24:10–16) Couldn't we just burn them to death at a private family affair like we do with people who sleep with their in-laws? (Lev. 20:14)

I know you have studied these things extensively, so I am confident you can help.

Thank you again for reminding us that God's word is eternal and unchanging.

Your devoted disciple
and adoring fan.[5]

Such tongue-in-cheek literalism is likely to delight those of us who believe in God's laughter. But for the many who believe that Scripture must be read by the book, as it were, serious adherence to elaborate rules leads to a lockstep, lifeless conformity. Surely God wants more from and for us. The Jesus of the Gospels, himself a Jew who knew the law, repeatedly says so to the law-bound Pharisees, as when he chides, "Well did Isaiah prophesy about you hypocrites, as it is written: 'This people honors me with their lips, but their hearts are far from me; in vain do they worship me, teaching as doctrines human precepts.' You disregard God's commandment but cling to human tradition" (Mark 7:6–8). Through his life as well as his teachings, Jesus subsumes the Mosaic code and all its offshoots under a pair of directives: Love God and love your neighbor. God wants not a rote response to a set of rules but a lively and all-consuming love. If we can achieve this (and most of us can do so only sporadically and with great concentration), our innate perverse desire to sin will dissolve, freeing us to do God's work in the world.

And will we then have achieved immortality? Of course not. The death that comes into the world through sin is not biological but spiritual. Whenever I separate myself from God through a failure to love, my spirit languishes until through the grace of God, who never ceases to love me, even at my worst, I repent and return to my calling. But even after I've recognized my sin, confessed it to God, and achieved by one means or another an attitude of true contrition, I can't just congratulate myself and get on with my life. Something in that life urged or at least enabled me to transgress. Unless I plan to remain trapped in a squirrel-cage of wrongdoing and regret, I will have to live differently from now on. Inevitably, being human, I'm going to sin again, but it had better be a different sin next time. Moral maturity requires that I learn from my errors in order to increase my reverence for and devotion to the Holy.

Jesus names some of the disciplines that characterize a penitent life. Of these, fasting directs itself toward the individual sinner, using self-denial either as a punishment for misdeeds or, as in my case, a means toward mindfulness of and remorse for them. Prayer may focus either inward toward the self and its relationship to God or outward on behalf of others. Almsgiving is purely other-directed, an emptying of the self in service to the needs of both neighbors and strangers. In maturity, the sinner recognizes that just as the individual may stray from God, so may society at large. In order to be reconciled with God, each of us is called to make restitution for both personal and social wrongdoing. Almsgiving means more than merely writing out a check to a favorite charity, I think. It means adopting a conscientious way of life that expresses a caring relationship with the whole of God's creation. Salvation is not an individual matter, and Jesus Christ is nobody's *personal* savior but the savior of all the world, redeeming us through his insistent teachings, the very ones that caused him to be crucified in the first place. In this sense he may be said to have died for us. Until the well-being of every person everywhere is fostered according to his instruction, we are all lost.

The temptation of Jesus early in his ministry illustrates the fully mature moral response to which we are all called. Every detail in the account contrasts with Eve and Adam's trial. No longer are we shown a verdant garden, where every craving except one can be satisfied, but rather a desert wilderness. Instead of a sly serpent, we have a featureless "devil" as the tempter. Eve succumbs to the serpent's blandishments and eats, even though she is not hungry; Jesus, though famished, resists. Most significantly, both quote the word of God to their tempters, but whereas Eve dithers and then permits the serpent to persuade her that God is wrong, Jesus relies firmly on Scripture to counter each of the devil's offers. Eve acts against God's orders and in her own interests: to please her palate and to gain knowledge. Jesus's resistance is entirely contrary to his interests. Not only could he allay the hunger gnawing at him after forty days without food, but he could find out for certain whether he is indeed the Son of God and, if so, he could possess untold worldly power. Many of us would settle for a great deal less. But Jesus has spent his time in the wilderness well. His vision is clear and focused not on his personal appetites but on right action.

Perhaps we cannot attain the moral perfection ascribed to the Jesus of the Gospels, but we are not morally helpless either. Time after time, we are given opportunities to choose, as he was. We can be guided by principles we have developed through contemplating his words: "You shall love God with all your heart, with all your soul, and with all your mind. This is the greatest and the first commandment. The second is like it: You shall love your neighbor as yourself." (Matt. 22:37–39) That's it. Nothing esoteric. These precepts are observed in many spiritual traditions, including secular ones. Each time we refuse to use others to advance our own ends and instead meet their needs, each time we forgive actions (even our own) that at first glance seem "unforgivable" and embrace the people (even ourselves) who seem "unlovable," we have drawn a step closer to the Holy.

Good news! Your sins have always already been forgiven! This is the message Jesus came into the world to bring us: God loves us so dearly that, purely through grace and not through any merit we possess, God accepts us and cherishes us without condition. You are not personally required to follow a particular religious figure and practice, only the precepts taught by that one. Doing so may help you to develop spiritually, but it can also ossify your soul, especially if you believe that yours is the only route to holiness and any deviation from it will doom the wanderer to eternal suffering. As the meditation master, teacher, and artist Chögyam Trungpa says in a widely quoted passage: "Walking the spiritual path is a very subtle process; it is not something to jump into naively. There are numerous sidetracks which lead to a distorted, ego-centered version of spirituality; we can deceive ourselves into thinking we are developing spiritually when instead we are strengthening our egocentricity through spiritual techniques."[6] Sin and salvation are not about you as an individual but about you in relationship. To live blamelessly, you do not even have to believe in the God who embraces you. All that's required of you is to do justice, and to love kindness, and to walk humbly. If you think this rule lets you off lightly, you haven't tried it yet.

I don't think I began to grasp all-forgiving love until I became a parent and learned that, no matter how badly my children might act and how I might condemn their actions, I could not cease to love them. I could correct them. I could require them to make restitution for any harm they caused. I could encourage them to repent their actions and refrain from repeating them. But I could not withhold my love. In my son Matthew's early adolescence, I received a call from a University of Arizona police officer, who told me, "We have your son here, and you need to come sign for him." He and another boy, spying an opening in the ceiling of a university sports center, had wormed through it and ridden their skateboards over the rafters until the racket attracted the attention of a startled security guard. I dutifully sprang him, and his father and I accompanied him to meet with a juvenile justice officer, who assigned him twenty-five hours of community service at a local soup kitchen. I was exasperated beyond measure by his folly—and by myriad more in the years that followed—in part because I loved immoderately this being I had created, whom I had tried to prepare and must slowly relinquish to his own choices and their consequences. And I'm only human!

Since then, I have watched my daughter attain the same enlightenment, as I learned from a note she wrote to me:

> Dear Mom: On this Mother's Day when I am an almost mother, I wanted to let you know how much I appreciate you for being my mother. I realize now that no one can really understand the

bond a mother feels with her child except another mother. Not even the child, as much as she may love her mother, can understand.

As I feel the baby inside me now, I imagine how you must have felt feeling me move and grow stronger, imagining what I might look like or what I might become. Also, as I worry about our baby (everything from whether he'll be healthy to how to raise him as a good person), I realize all the worries I must have given you. I want to thank you for raising me well and for continuing to love and support me through the years.

Have a Happy Mother's Day! I love you!

—Anne.

Reading this note in the hubbub of a restaurant, I could not have been gladder that, thirty-one years earlier and without much heed for the consequences, I committed myself to motherhood.

When Anne was born, I was nearly ten years younger than she was when she wrote it, and although I surely worried about her health, I doubt that I knew enough to have qualms about her goodness. One quality conferred by a Calvinist upbringing in a village on the north shore of Massachusetts in the 1950s was a confidence, perhaps even a conviction, that rectitude was something of a birthright. As long as a man worked steadily at the managerial or professional level and returned home every evening to a spotless house and a hot meal and two scrubbed children ready for a night-night kiss; as long as a woman confined her out-of-the-house activities to service and social clubs with other like-minded women; as long as the children attended school regularly, joined the Scouts, didn't go "parking" and get each other "in trouble" (or, if they did, married quickly and quietly); as long as the family, unbroken by divorce, showed up at the large white Congregational church on the village green every Sunday—they were all, as a matter of course, the right kind of people.

Such a setting, snug but also smug, where good was something you were (or weren't), not something you did, fostered an almost ludicrous naïveté. My idea of living on the edge entailed a visit to my aunt's house in Boston, where some of the guests might wear long black stockings and write poetry. I had never heard of heroin, abortion, domestic violence, homelessness; we gave our castoffs to Goodwill, but I had never met anyone whose nakedness they might clothe. Moral distinctions seemed pretty plain. Those who lived as we did were good. Those who lived otherwise (in other words, most of the world) were not good—not necessarily evil but certainly benighted, their hope of redemption lying in their becoming more like us. Small wonder that I didn't fret over my baby's moral health: simply by virtue of being my daughter, she was destined to become a good person.

In the wake of the Vietnam War, which drove home for many of us the discontinuity between righteousness and right, when I began to relinquish the Mosaic certitude that I was among God's chosen as long as I obeyed the stone-carved rules, I felt drawn more and more strongly toward the essential message of the Gospel: that God loves all creation, not in a mawkish fashion but fiercely, fixedly, without restraint, expecting much yet forgiving each failure, suffering with us in defeat, promising that we can do better next time, refusing to abandon or destroy what She has made no matter how blemished it may seem to our limited vision.

In other words, Jesus spoke literally: God's love epitomizes parental love, and goodness is indeed the birthright of my children —my daughter and later her brother—in ways I once could not have conceived. Because Anne is not a Christian, she will have to find a different (and, as I imagine it, a more difficult) route to the recognition that goodness is not a state into which she can draw her children by either instruction or inspiration. Nor is it a quantity that she can pour into them until they are filled and finished. Rather, it is a journey with many way stations. Since staying out of trouble is a wholly inadequate indicator of goodness, her heart may be broken, perhaps many times over, as they stumble—and she, too—along the way. What will get them all through has little to do with propriety. What will get them through to the point that they can celebrate one another as good-people-in-the-works is the passion and intensity now stirring in her—all we can know firsthand of God's love.

The effect of sin is to create a chasm between the self and God-as-parent so wide and black that we forget that God waits for us, sorrowfully but with infinite patience, on the other side. God is not harmed by our sin—God cannot be harmed—but grieves over the harm we do ourselves and one another. Through repentance and restoration, we can close the distance between us and be reconciled, literally brought together again. Oddly, through our sin we can thus be drawn closer to God, participating more fully in the mercy that flows from God through us into all creation. All God asks of us—and this for our own sakes, not for God's—is that we accept Jesus's teaching and put it to work in our lives. If we take care of one another, we are saved.

ENOUGH *IS* ENOUGH

We pray to the great Spiritual Power in which we live and move and have our being. We pray that we may at all times keep our minds open to new ideas and shun dogma; that we may grow in our understanding of the nature of all living beings and our connectedness with the natural world; that we may become ever more filled with generosity of spirit and true compassion and love for all life; that we may strive to heal the hurts that we have inflicted on nature and control our greed for material things, knowing that our actions are harming our natural world and the future of our children; that we may value each and every human being for who he is, for who she is, reaching to the spirit that is within, knowing the power of each individual to change the world.

from DR. JANE GOODALL'S
prayer for world peace

A few years ago, for the first time in my life, I prepared an income-tax return. This was doubtless a foolish use of my time. After all, the year before we had shoved a mess of papers at a tax preparer and then paid him a mere $75 to make sense of them. I spent at least twenty-four hours just initiating myself into the arcana of TurboTax (which is not so highly charged as the name implies), so even at minimum wage I'd be a bad bargain. That year, however, the tax preparer had made a careless error. "Well, I can make a mistake for free," I told my husband with what would turn out to be baseless bravado, "and even though I'm a mathematical booby, I'm a whiz with computers. I'll do them." George didn't hoot, though he did look a little dubious as I fired up the computer. Some weeks later I sat back, utterly wrung out, while the printer spat forth page after complicated page of my handiwork. For weeks afterward, I waited for the IRS to come cart me off to prison for the terrible botch I was sure I had made.

Despite fatigue and apprehension, I was glad I had undertaken this task. For one thing, in thirty-four years of marriage I had never before gained such a clear view of our finances—an unconscionable lapse in a woman who claims that hers is a partnership of equals. Now a bit of the murk had lifted. For another, the exercise confirmed for me the conviction George and I have long held that, even though the combined incomes of a retired high-school English teacher and a wheelchair user on Social Security would strike many as paltry, we have all we need.

This sense of sufficiency can be hard to come by in a society premised on scarcity. Immigrants will come and confiscate our livelihoods, we fret; poor people will suck society dry with their needs for subsidized shelter and nourishment; pollution will destroy the very air we breathe and the water we drink; small children will bleed away our scant fiscal resources with their demands for food, medicine, education. People living on the street go wet and hungry while we save for a rainy day. The certainty that there is never enough of anything to go around condemns us to a state of chronic anxiety.

I once had a friend, for example, who worried that he had only $30,000 in his savings account. (He confided this as though I knew what it was to have a $30,000 savings account.) When his sister and brother invited him to share a rented cottage in Cornwall with their elderly mother for a couple of weeks, he decided he couldn't afford such a costly holiday. In frail health, his mother seemed unlikely to live many more years, and if the money were mine, I would have squandered some of those savings this minute, the one scarcity I readily acknowledge being time. I call such "extravagances" deposits in the memory bank. Clearly, I am the grasshopper to my friend's ant, and it will serve me right to end up in the poorhouse for my improvidence.

But I am not in the poorhouse at this moment, and this moment is the one in which I live. If the poorhouse comes later, then I'll live in it.

Our society would unravel altogether if we stopped believing in scarcity. Unless one perceives a lack, one won't spend one's money to fill it, and getting and spending have come to seem the source rather than the waste of our powers. To the blandishments of consumerism I am as vulnerable as anyone else who picks up a magazine or flips on the television. I want. I want. I covet a computer twice as fast as the one I use, even though no microchip can force me to write at other than my accustomed glacial pace. I yearn for a power wheelchair that would climb stairs and raise me to eye level when everyone around me is standing. Then there's this adorable wheelchair-adapted PT Cruiser . . . I browse catalogs in order to find new things to want. Desire runs amok.

I can forgive myself these cravings, aware that they are merely symptoms of a kind of social soul-sickness rather than needs that must be filled if I am to live "the good life." I have—while too many do not—a modest but comfortable house, more to eat than my aging metabolism requires, a closet bursting with clothes, a serviceable vehicle, medical and dental insurance. I am not entitled to any of these. I just got lucky. Many of us living through the second half of the twentieth century have enjoyed privileges undreamed of by any of our ancestors and, thanks to the heedlessness with which we sucked up the resources required for so much warmth and light and nourishment, unlikely to be available to our scions.

I repudiate the Calvinist values of my forebears, who viewed earned wealth as no impediment to virtue, because the Jesus of the Gospels who is my teacher speaks plainly on the subject: "You cannot serve God and mammon" (Matt. 6:24). I find shocking the notion of "Christian economics," in which "God is an entrepreneur" and "the goal of God's free enterprise system is to reward hard work and punish slothfulness."[1] I know too many poor hard workers and too many indolent clippers of coupons to believe that the system enacts divine will rather than simply justifying greed and insensitivity. God did not set it up so that five of the ten richest people in America belong to Wal-Mart's Walton family, and in 2004 "Scott Lee Jr., Wal-Mart's chief executive, was paid $17.5 million. That is, every two weeks Mr. Lee was paid about as much as his average employee will earn in a lifetime."[2] The system is rigged — but not by God.

If I must worry about material possessions, glut threatens my well-being, not privation. My things distract me and distance me from the realities of most of the earth's population, and as long as I have a morsel more to eat than a child in drought-ridden Malawi, through whom God has also entered the world, I live in sin. This is not the personal sin that seems to preoccupy the majority of Christians. Truth to tell, God isn't unduly interested in that sort of sin, which is easy enough for the alert individual to recognize, confess, and correct. Rather, it is systemic sin, a way of constructing the world that perpetuates, indeed necessitates, inequity.

In my part of the world, for instance, farmers from Mexico and Central America who used to subsist on the corn they grew now cross into the United States without documentation and trudge through miles of hostile desert. Often they do so repeatedly, caught by the Border Patrol and returned to Mexico time and again. Those who do not give up, and those who do not die of dehydration, either hypo- or hyperthermia depending on the time of year, or snakebite, make their way into the pesticide-laden fields of growers throughout the Southwest and beyond. There, for wages so low that U.S. workers won't accept them, they pick the lettuce I just ate in my Caesar salad and the grapes for the Chardonnay I washed it down with. While they are traveling north, they meet trains carrying containers labeled Archer Daniels Midland, each one stuffed with cheap, genetically modified corn to be dumped at prices for which no farmer could live, the profits from which will earn stockholders 8.5 cents per share. I'm no economist, as my tax agonies make plain, and I don't know what strategy could begin to untangle this scandalous mess. But I'm sure it doesn't involve sitting back and congratulating myself that my creature comforts are either God's reward for my exemplary behavior or a sign of my preordained heavenly bliss.

Nowhere does the Jesus of the Gospels say, "Grab all you can get and hang on to it for dear life." If anything, his attitude toward possessions reflects the insouciance of an itinerant teacher whose needs are customarily met by the households he visits. "I tell you, do not worry about your life, what you will eat (or drink), or about your body, what you will wear. Is not life more than food and the body more than clothing?" he tells his followers (Matt. 6:25). When he sends them out as missionaries, his instructions dismiss material concerns: "Carry no money bag, no sack, no sandals; and greet no one along the way. Into whatever house you enter, first say, 'Peace to this household.' If a peaceful person lives there, your peace will rest on him; but if not, it will return to you. Stay in the same house and eat and drink what is offered to you, for the laborer deserves his payment. Do not move about from one house to another. Whatever town you enter and they welcome you, eat what is set before you" (Luke 10:4–8).

Jesus rejects not so much possessions themselves but the desire for and attachment to them that eats up attention that would better be devoted to God's work. "Take care to guard against all greed," he cautions, "for though one may be rich, one's life does not consist of possessions" (Luke 12:15). Things require so much effort to accumulate and house and maintain and protect—and then, just like the rich man tearing down one barn to build a bigger one, you may die at any moment, spiritually empty-handed. Instead, he says, "Sell your belongings and give alms. Provide money bags for yourselves that do not wear out, an inexhaustible treasure in heaven that no thief can reach nor moth destroy. For where your treasure is, there also will your heart be" (Luke 12:33–34). This is the queerest entrepreneurial attitude I've ever come across.

In one of his thornier parables, Jesus concludes: "For to everyone who has, more will be given and he will grow rich; but from the one who has not, even what he has will be taken away" (Matt. 25: 29). On the face of it, this appears to be little more than a cynical appraisal of the world's colossal unfairness. Still, Jesus is never depicted as a cynic, and Matthew may well have drafted this passage with the eschatological intent commentators have ascribed to it. Since I don't believe in reward and punishment after death, however, this observation as originally framed yields me precious little insight. But the marvel of the Gospels lies in their capacity to be reframed in ways that illuminate the full range of human experience, and so these words resonate for me here. If you believe yourself richly blessed, they suggest, then your life will seem to brim over with goodness; but if you feel deprived—of money, prestige, affection, control, whatever you value most—you will squander your energies bemoaning your lacks and defending what little you perceive yourself to have.

The issue of sufficiency, then, involves interpretation, which is hardly so simple as the old glass-half-full-or-half-empty conceit would make it. My friend, a devoted son, would never deny his mother anything he thought he could provide; for him the threat of impoverishment arises not from selfishness or negativism but from a genuine terror that the wolf is at the door and only his thrift can debar its dripping fangs. And yet another friend, almost eighty and in constant arthritic pain, who lives in public housing and wears cast-off clothing, quietly and without apparent qualm gives away every penny she can spare—and probably more. "I came that they may have life, and have it abundantly," Jesus says (John 10:10). He offers an abundance of *life*, which "does not consist in the abundance of possessions" (Luke 12:15). We may have it abundantly—if we will.

The celebration of abundance is stipulated from our earliest cultural roots, when Yahweh "gave us this land, a land flowing with milk and honey," Deuteronomy records (26:9–10). The phrase reveals that the people to whom Moses laid out God's law belonged to an agrarian society, keeping goats and bees. The "first fruit of the ground" they offered to God might have been, quite literally, dates and figs and olives, as well as grain to make the bread by which alone no one must live. By today's standards, theirs would have seemed a meager existence: a brief life devoted to cultivating crops and rearing livestock in a semiarid land. Yet Moses's injunction is to "rejoice" in the harvest. Not to measure it. Not to grumble that it's too small to feed the growing number of mouths at the table. Not to fret that next year you might not fare as well, a hard freeze killing off your grapevines or an infestation of locusts chomping up your wheat. Just to delight in what the land has produced and to thank God for it.

How differently we live now that we're bombarded from every side with messages that whatever we have is too small, too old, too shabby, too boring. We can't be permitted simply to rejoice in our possessions or else we wouldn't want more of them. "More," not "enough," is the operant word, driving the mad but not mysterious cycle of production, acquisition, disposal, replacement...God doesn't enter this loop. God might be thought to send a parching wind that shrivels the first sprouts or a rain that rescues the crop at the last moment, but Bill Gates sends the software that keeps our lives humming along.

No one wants to go back to the subsistence living of biblical times, and we couldn't even if we wanted to. But we can't sustain our current rapacious habits, either. We need to bring forward into our own world the sense of sufficiency, even abundance, felt by those who believed they had been given "a land of milk and honey." We need to cultivate in ourselves the habit of gratitude for the plenty we have.

Moses instructs the Israelites not just to feel good about the crops they've raised and gathered in, not even just to sing God's praises for providing the land and the conditions that resulted in such plenty, but actually to put some of the produce in a basket woven of peeled willow twigs and take it to the priest as an offering back to God (Deut. 26:2–4). This is to be the *first* fruit, mind you. No hanging back to see if there will be a surplus and offering the leftovers. Through this offering, Moses says, "you shall rejoice in all the good which the LORD your God has given to you and to your house" (Deut. 26:11). And what would have become of the offering, I wonder. Perhaps it was left to rot, but such waste seems unlikely. Might not the priest have taken it, to feed himself and his family or to give to the poor?

In any case, the message seems clear: Although gratitude for God's bounty puts us into right relation with our possessions, it doesn't fulfill our responsibility for them. As Moses enjoins, we need to give some of them away. And not our junk, either. Real goods for which people might have some use. But no act seems harder in a society premised on scarcity rather than abundance. If we believe that no matter how much we own, more will make us safer from any possible want, then we can't bear to part with the least thing. We need to practice feeling safe when *others* have more.

When it comes to material possessions, I've had an easier time developing a sense of their abundance than I've had overcoming my attachment to them. In this process, essential for spiritual ease, I've had plenty of instruction, none more strenuous than the teachings of Bentley Barker, the Labrador retriever who joined our household some years ago as a nine-month-old puppy, throwing all of us—but especially Lucky Pup and the two geriatric cats who lived with us then—into a perpetual uproar. Within a couple of weeks, Bentley had demolished a pair of spectacles; two wicker wastebaskets and a laundry basket; an album of family photographs lovingly assembled by my mother; a bromeliad, a begonia, and a feather bush; and a friend's favorite novel, long out of print—to name the items that spring immediately to mind. One night my husband returned from a quick errand to find a copy of Barbara Woodhouse's *No Bad Dogs*, toothmarks in one corner, propped against the patio door as though to remind him of its forgiving philosophy before he discovered the coffee grounds strewn across the kitchen floor. The house resonated with a sorrowful refrain: "Oh, Bentley Barker, what have you done? What have you done now?"

None of this, it turns out, mattered very much. There was a time —most of my life, in fact—when such a series of mishaps would have triggered hysterics, fury, perhaps even a major depressive episode. That time seems to have passed without much notice. Now I greet each fiasco coolly, quizzically, exasperation tempered by amusement. "Ah, so that's what happens next," I say to myself, simply letting each thing go. Possess nothing, experience has taught me, that you cannot bear to live without. Such resignation might signal melancholy, I suppose, but I recall reading somewhere that a depressive's difficulty lies in the inability to let go, not in easy relinquishment. And Bentley, oh Bentley, his mustache and beard now silvery, who has left behind most of his puppyhood (and a few of our furnishings)—one day I shall have to let even him go.

Letting go of feelings is hard and relinquishing people, of course, hardest of all. I am reminded of my mother some years back, fuming because an aunt and uncle had asked my sister and her husband to drive them the twenty-five miles to our Christmas gathering, a service my parents had grown accustomed to receiving

themselves. "They have absolutely no consideration for other people," Mother sputtered, and I murmured sympathetically. Always
in charge ("an iron fist in a velvet glove," she used to call my father's
mother, but her own glove has sometimes been forged of chain
mail), she seemed increasingly to respond to the complexities that
escaped her grasp—her beloved brother had just died of prostate
cancer, her husband had developed a second skin cancer, a daughter and a granddaughter had incurable degenerative diseases—with
anger, often deflected onto tangential issues.

Even a few years ago, Mother would have made sarcastic re-
marks about Their Royal Highnesses, no doubt, but without openly
acknowledging her irritation. I can speak with some assurance here
because this was also my emotional style until my daughter told
me one day that my greatest flaw was my indirectness: a family
trait, perhaps even a cultural one, since we descended directly from
the Puritans who settled the communities in which we continued
to live. In our household, any outpouring of sentiment, even delight, was dismissed as "dramatics," and overt hostility, even the sort
that bursts out between siblings no matter how close they are, was
quickly quashed. Other people might crow or wail or shout, but We
Knew Better.

Although Mother could now admit to anger, it still constituted
an unruliness to be mastered, as her next comment made plain:
"I've got to get hold of myself, or nobody will like me very much."
Socially, anger tends to be viewed as a menace. Just look at the verbs
we use with it: "erupt," "explode," "blow up," "boil over." *Keep a lid
on it,* we caution, even though, as anyone who's overheated a pres-
sure cooker can attest, the tight lid is exactly what causes the device
to spew bits of potato from floor to ceiling.

"Don't worry about that," I replied. "We all know what it's like
to be angry. Just open up to it, really feel it, and then let it flow on
out and away." The process, a sort of spiritual exercise that has

grown out of what my husband and I half-humorously call our Zen Catholicism, sounds so simple put into words. But how hard it is to part with righteous indignation. It feels so, well, *right!*

I tend to learn life's lessons only through tedious drill, but the one about anger came to me all at once. During Mass one Saturday evening several years ago, when George neglected to hand me a hymnal, I was suffused by irritation, which masked, I suppose now, the dread that choked me throughout his cancer treatment. From long experience, I knew that an evening of sullen silence stretched before us. Although I didn't want to pollute whatever time might be left us, I felt mired in a pattern thirty years in the making. Having heard traditional Catholics refer to offering some distress up to God, I decided to give this puzzling practice a go. "Well, God, I'm certainly stuck," I said. "Can you help me get over this anger?" Nothing much seemed to happen, but when it was time to depart in peace, I said to George, "Grocery shopping seems like a bleak activity for a Saturday night," the only time during the week he could squeeze it in. "Why don't we catch a bite and then do it together?" He shops more efficiently and economically, no doubt, when I'm not spinning up and down the aisles in a whirlwind of impulses, but we spent a pleasant evening anyway.

Although in my clumsy prayer I had asked only for a tranquil evening, not a lifelong transformation, perhaps that's what I got: not immunity from anger (and complaint and jealousy and all the other mean-spirited responses to life's events that sicken the soul) but the belief that whereas the great Working Out I know as God is utterly beyond my comprehension and control, my attitude is not. Acceptance feels more soothing than anger; rejoicing delights me as moaning never can.

"Oh well, I don't suppose it really matters." Mother sounded less than persuaded.

"No, it doesn't," I agreed. "What matters is being together for Christmas." What more could I tell her? I certainly couldn't advise her to offer her anger up to God. She'd given up on God long ago, beginning perhaps with my father's sudden death, at Christmastime, when they were both twenty-eight. With Mother I could speak out of my faith but not about it. Like children everywhere, especially those who have lost one parent, I feared the loss of the other and with her all hope of survival. I always felt anxious when my mother seemed out of sorts. I can still recall my awkward attempts, as a child, to comfort her when she was ill or seemed downhearted, and I have borne vestiges of that child into adulthood. I wanted to please Mother. I wanted to make her happy. But maturity teaches that another's happiness lies beyond control. I guessed I'd just have to offer Mother and all my complicated feelings about her up to God. And then, less than a year later, I had to do so forever.

"My life is a lesson in losses," I wrote in one of my earliest essays, with more bravado than confidence; perhaps the lesson has begun to take hold. Thanks to multiple sclerosis, one thing after another has been wrenched from my life—dancing, driving, walking, working—and I have learned neither to yearn after them nor to dread further deprivation but to attend to what I have. I don't mean that I forget them. On the contrary. Letting go is different. In the teaching of Thich Nat Hanh, this is called mindfulness, and it seems unattainable as long as one frets over possessions, whether intellectual or material. In meditation, not by accident are the hands held loosely, palms up. In this position they cannot grasp, only cradle or release.

I have reached the point of preparing to release myself into death. This desire for an end turns out to be sharply different from the compulsion toward suicide that haunted me during the many years I was depressed. For one thing, I have become, as I predicted in one of my very early essays, too crippled to kill myself. But neither do I want to anymore. On the contrary, I want to live forever! I recite Edna St. Vincent Millay's words, "Oh world, I cannot hold thee close enough!" as I gaze across my backyard at the silly lesser gold-finches flashing citrine and emerald as they twirl upside down on their perches to pick at their thistle seed. Under the feather bush, a fat lizard does push-ups. The hibiscuses, continuing their struggle against this arid climate, have started to bloom again. Today three red ones have flowered at once: one, called Fire Engine, has a saucer-size blossom the color of flame; another, San Diego Red, is scarlet with recurved petals; the third, aptly named Raspberry Breeze, is a mass of ruffles. Even on a single plant, the flowers are never identical. Fire Engine's current offering has an uncharacteristic kink in the stamen. They seem designed to manifest the infinite variability of the cosmos.

Nor does my burgeoning delight in the least of the world's gifts confine itself to comfort and aesthetic pleasure. I embrace the strange and even the downright ugly. A couple of weeks ago, on a trip to Brooklyn, I had an encounter with a walrus in the New York Aquarium. As I sat close to the underwater viewing window, a walrus swam up to the glass, head down, gazing at me with large dark eyes while rumbles and squeaks issued from beneath a dense moustache. Rapt, I spent several minutes listening and replying; when I moved to another window, the walrus followed me and continued our conversation. This was empty of content, at least for me, but seemed to represent contact for us both. I have never felt happier.

A couple of days later, George and I meandered from our not-many-starred hotel down to the river, through a particularly un-lovely area of largely derelict warehouses, my wheelchair jouncing over broken sidewalks and potholed streets. "Oh, George," I said in the tremorous voice such rough terrain elicits, "is there anything I don't find interesting?" No. In my immobility, I have become absorbed by my surroundings, so that I hardly know anymore where I leave off and they begin. I am perhaps a walrus. The older I grow, the closer to shedding my human form and consciousness for some unknown otherwise, the more I cherish the moments left to me and the sadder and more mystified I feel that the world's wonders will continue to unfold without me.

Since they will do so regardless of my willingness to let them go, the best I can do is ready myself for my leave-taking. A couple of years ago, visiting my daughter and her family when they lived on the Zuni reservation, where Eric practiced medicine, we took the children to a large playground, where at a distance I watched them play on the swings and slides. I have become the world's witness. As a large thunderstorm boiled up over the mesas and headed our way, it occurred to me that, sitting in the middle of an empty field, I could be struck by lightning. "If I am," I asked, "will I die happy?" I needn't have asked, so quick and firm was my response. Since that epiphanic moment, watching the signs of my immortality romp and sway, preparing to leave them, I have tried to live in such a way that, if the question ripples through my mind, as it often does, I can always answer, "Yes!"

Several years ago, one of George's students fashioned for me a large lizard of black wrought iron, which looked splendid in the play of light against my creamy studio wall. "It will be stolen," my daughter declared, knowing that the university area where we then lived attracted thieves, and she was right. In my outrage, I wished I could put a curse on it so that it would poison the life of the thief and of whomever he sold it to for drug money. But I had loved the lizard that graced my wall. How could I imagine its bearing evil to anyone? So I put a blessing on it instead, that wherever it fetched up, it bestow on its new owner as much pleasure as it had brought me. In its place, a muralist painted an enormous, vibrant image of La Virgen de Guadalupe, who remained there until the many-tentacled University of Arizona bought the aging little structure and tore it down.

Bless what you have, she taught me. Bless what has gone. Bless whatever may come next.

RISEN? RISEN INDEED!

I simply do not see how strict inerrantists can stay sane. Because they believe that the Bible contains no contradictions but rather a perfect morality without ethical defects, they have to accept the wildest stories and make the most far-fetched judgments. First, Yahweh slays all the firstborn of the Egyptians, and then he drowns the entire Egyptian army; eight chapters later, he thunderously prohibits killing, engraving his decree in stone. Are we to conclude that he has one set of rules for himself and another for human beings? That doesn't seem a very fair arrangement, but okay, let's say that's just how it is. We are enjoined not to kill. Note that the verb has no object. As a result, we are not forbidden to kill this, that, or the other; we are forbidden to kill at all. In the next couple of chapters, we are commanded to kill murderers, children who strike or curse their parents, kidnappers, buggers of beasts, witches, and worshipers of any god but Yahweh, to name but a few.

Extraordinary events abound: Very many very dry bones rattle together, rise up from the desert floor, and return to life; one boy slays a giant, and three others emerge unburnt from a fiery furnace; women conceive in very old age or as virgins; men scale mountains to converse with God and dead prophets. To believe that these incidents actually took place defies reason; but to say that God made them take place moves beyond irrationality into lunacy. Not all such beliefs are necessarily bad, although they sometimes do lead to such very bad behavior as burning or stoning women to death.

They're just, factually speaking, nonsensical. It's as though I were convinced that a little person with furry feet really did undertake to carry a ring through the dangerous wilderness into a dark land and there hurl it into an abyss of fire. No harm done—but I'd miss the underlying resonances of Tolkien's story.

Except that all too often, harm *is* done. People who believe that the stories of their tradition, told orally or in writing, constitute factual reporting and instruction dictated by a divine being have little tolerance for stories that deviate from "God's word" even slightly. Instead of seeing that the stories arising in other traditions attempt to shape the same mysterious and ineffable Whole into accounts that human intelligence can contemplate, and that each may offer glimmers of insight others have failed to illuminate, believers decree their visions to be constitutionally different from any others, declare theirs "true" and "good" and others "false" and even "evil," and set about eradicating all who believe otherwise.

Here is a part of the elaborate Hopi creation myth:

"I am Tawa," sang the Sun God. "I am Light. I am Life. I am Father of all that shall ever come."

"I am Kokyanwuhti," the Spider Woman crooned. "I receive Light and nourish Life. I am Mother of all that shall ever come."

"Many strange thoughts are forming in my mind—beautiful forms of birds to float in the Above, of beasts to move upon the Earth and fish to swim in the Waters," intoned Tawa.

"Now let these things that move in the Thought of Tawa appear," chanted Spider Woman, while with her slender fingers she caught up clay from beside her and made the Thoughts of Tawa take form. One by one she shaped them and laid them aside—but they breathed not nor moved.

"We must do something about this," said Tawa. "It is not good that they lie thus still and quiet. Each thing that has a form must also have a spirit. So now, my beloved, we must make a mighty Magic."

They laid a white blanket over the many figures, a cunningly woven woolen blanket, fleecy as a cloud, and made a mighty incantation over it, and soon the figures stirred and breathed.

"Now, let us make ones like unto you and me, so that they may rule over and enjoy these lesser creatures," sang Tawa, and Spider Woman shaped the Thoughts into woman and man figures like unto their own. But after the blanket magic had been made, the figures remained inert. So Spider Woman gathered them all in her arms and cradled them, while Tawa bent his glowing eyes upon them. The two now sang the magic Song of Life over them, and at last each human figure breathed and lived.[1]

The details differ—the Holy explicitly comprises both male and female, for example, and the creatures are sung into being—but they are no more far-fetched than a man being shaped out of dust and a woman formed from his rib. In another account, a single cell splits, multiplies, develops into jellyfish, newts, loons, panthers, bonobos, us. One of these tales lends itself to rational study and the others are articles of faith, but all arise from and in diverse ways satisfy our urge to understand human origins.

Even though I do not believe that the Bible reports actual events, I sometimes find it useful to reliteralize the Gospel narratives as a starting point for visiting and revisiting their import. This is especially true during Holy Week, which recounts a tale of joy and suffering and joy through suffering which I find both chastening and instructive. As this season begins again, I'll narrate the details of the Easter story as I recall them. I think I'll tell the tale straight through, without referring to texts or critiques, to find out which details have stayed with me through years and years of hearing and reading it.

*

Five days before his death, Jesus and his followers went to Jerusalem to celebrate Passover. He sent a couple of people ahead to a place where they would find a donkey and a white colt. "If anyone asks why you are taking them," he instructed, "tell them the Master has need of them." As he approached the city astride the donkey, people who had heard of him ran out and ushered him in, strewing palm fronds and their clothes in front of him and shouting, "Hosanna!" At the temple, he found money changers and vendors selling doves and goats for sacrifice; furious at seeing a holy place given over to commerce, he upturned the tables and drove the merchants away. The group from Galilee didn't stay in Jerusalem, however, but at a place nearby.

A day or two later, he sent a couple of people (probably not the same ones — he had a lot of followers) to tell a man to prepare a room where he and his friends could share a Passover meal. At that meal, when he blessed the ritual bread and wine, he told the company that these were his body and his blood and that whenever they performed the same ritual, they were to remember him. He also told them that one among them would betray him, and Judas Iscariot sneaked out. Jesus told Peter that before the next morning, Peter would three times deny knowing Jesus. Later that evening, they went to a garden, Gethsemane, and he asked the disciples to keep watch while he prayed, but at least twice he found them asleep. He prayed, "Father, if you will, please take this cup from me. If you will not, then I accept it." A group of soldiers then arrived, led by Judas, who kissed him on the cheek to identify him to them. Peter grabbed a sword and sliced off the ear of one of them, but Jesus chided him and mended the ear. With Jesus under arrest, they all trooped back into Jerusalem, where Jesus was taken to the palace of Pontius Pilate. Peter stayed in the courtyard, where he protested three times before cockcrow that he did not know the man who had been arrested.

Inside the palace, Pilate questioned Jesus: "Are you the king of the Jews?" Jesus replied, "You have said so." Apparently this was not too inflammatory a response, because Pilate went out and said to the crowd that had gathered, "I can find no fault with this good man." Nevertheless, they yelled, "Crucify him!" In accordance with the practice of freeing one Jewish prisoner at Passover time, Pilate offered to release Jesus and execute another revolutionary, Barabas, but they kept shouting for Jesus. Pilot acquiesced, washing his hands publicly to show that he did not take responsibility for their choice. Meanwhile, Roman soldiers stripped Jesus, wrapped him in a red cloak, put a crown of thorns on his head, and bowed mockingly: "All hail, king of the Jews." When they'd had their fun, they put his clothes back on and forced him to carry his own cross to the crucifixion site, Golgotha, Place of the Skull. When he could no longer bear its weight, they recruited a man known as Simon of Cyrene to carry it for him.

The soldiers tried to make him drink wine mixed with gall, which he refused, and took off his clothes, for which they cast lots. Then they nailed him to the cross, with other criminals at each side. One of these mocked him, but the other said, "Jesus, remember me when you come into your kingdom." Jesus assured him that they would be together in Paradise that very day. He hung there for about three hours. Above his head the Roman soldiers put a sign saying KING OF THE JEWS, and the crowd made fun of him, telling him to save himself if he was so powerful. All his friends ran away except his mother, a couple of other women, and "the disciple he loved," to whom he gave the care of his mother. At one point he cried out, "My God, my God, why have you forsaken me?"

At about three o'clock, he prayed, "Father, forgive them, for they know not what they do." Then he died. At this moment, there were thunder and lightning and an earthquake so severe that it "rent the veil of the temple." His body was taken down and given to a wealthy man, Joseph of Arimethea, who had him put into a tomb cut into a rocky hillside.

A couple of days later, early in the morning, some women went to the tomb and found it empty except for an angel, who said to them, "Why are you looking here? Jesus has risen and gone to Galilee. Tell the others to follow him there." Or else Mary Magdalene went alone and encountered a gardener, whom she did not at first recognize as Jesus. When she sought to embrace him, he said, "Touch me not, for I am not yet ascended to the Father." She ran to fetch Peter and another disciple, who were astonished to see the empty tomb. Jesus had risen from the stone slab, stripped away the winding-sheet, and vanished.

I have deliberately retold the story in this naive fashion—a mishmash of details from the Gospels and Paul, some only half-remembered, some perhaps embellished, together with a great many lacunae—because this resembles the way the Gospels themselves must have been composed. That is, the Gospel writers probably didn't witness these events or even interview anyone who had done so. There may well have been no eyewitnesses, no sympathetic ones anyway, since Mark reports that "all of the disciples left Jesus and ran away," although Peter followed far behind the arrested Jesus, he says, and some women watched the crucifixion from far away. (I do a lot better on details with the texts in front of me.) The writers had to rely upon stories handed down, probably orally, for decades, and anyone who has played the childhood game of Gossip knows just how unreliable such transmission can be.

Many years after the death of Jesus, Paul and the writers of the Gospels of Matthew, Mark, Luke, and John chose to record events and utterances that shaped the story to suit their own needs and the needs of the audiences for whom they were writing. Like me, they may even have introduced inventions (where on earth did that "*white* colt" come from?). Since none of the manuscripts exist in their original form, we must depend on translators and copyists, who make mistakes no matter how faithful they are. Although these were the only versions included in what came to be called the New Testament, for reasons that have nothing to do with their facticity, a number of others exist, among them the Gospel of Thomas, the Gospel of Philip, and the Gospel of Mary Magdalene. God did not inscribe any of them.

In short, the stories of Jesus's Passion and Resurrection may contain not a word of historical fact. If I don't believe that any of it actually happened, why do I tell myself the narrative again and again, all of it every year and a portion of it at least once a week? Partly out of habit, I suppose. This is my sixty-third Easter, and the events of the liturgical year have come to shape time's passage: the magical birth and the maturation of a Galilean carpenter into a teacher and healer whose radical preachings drew the attention of the Roman occupiers and led to his execution by crucifixion, a not uncommon fate for subversives. I know this story as well as I know my own. Indeed, through continual repetition, it has become integrated into the events of my life.

Each time the tale cycles round again, it echoes the endless movement of life into death into life through which we can glimpse eternity. Evidence abounds. Just a week or so ago, without any warning, the feather bush in my backyard shed all its leaves within a couple of days; a couple of days after that, green dots appeared along the newly naked branches; now it has leafed out and profuse buds have exploded into marble-size white puffs that will produce flat green seed pods. The dropped leaves have died and blown away, but the tree persists. Although one day this tree will desiccate and wither, throughout the Santa Cruz Valley others will sprout and flower and seed. This species will eventually die out, but others will evolve to take its place. Cessation and renewal: the fundamental rhythm of the All, enacted liturgically at Easter.

In the telling and retelling, I find reassurance. Jesus's last days offer insights into a range of experiences I too must have in some form or other. There is the transient triumph of his entrance into Jerusalem: some of the very people who shout "Hosanna!" will howl "Crucify him!" just days later. He takes his last meal in the company of those who love him. Yet he learns how fragile relationships can be: Judas betrays him; Peter denies him; his friends fall asleep in the midst of his agony. He prays to be spared, as we all do in crisis, and achieves resignation, as we may hope to do. Humiliated and tormented beyond endurance, he dies.

And rises again. This occurrence, steeped in mystery, offers an endless source of contemplation. No amount of repetition can exhaust it. Perhaps the body was never entombed but rather left to be eaten by wild dogs, as crucified bodies often were, ghoulish reminders of the fate waiting for enemies of the Roman state. Maybe, as D. H. Lawrence would have it, he was taken down too soon. Grave robbing was not uncommon. Maybe his body actually did begin to breathe again, and he shed his grave clothes, pushed aside the stone, and walked off to find his friends. Or perhaps those friends, gathered to grieve and remember him, felt his presence so strongly that he seemed to be among them still. Probably none of these farfetched theories are rooted in reality.

A lot of scholars suggest that an historical Jesus may not even have existed, although various sects grew up around figures like him at about that time, most notably John the Baptist. I think (purely intuitively, since I am no biblical scholar) that a man of extraordinary charisma—a mystic, prophet, teacher, and healer—must have existed, simply because I don't know how else to account for the power and durability of the belief system that eventually coalesced into Christianity. No fictional character has ever aroused and sustained a devotion that, over time, transformed into outright worship. Plenty of sects have come and gone, both then and thereafter, but this one persisted, grew into a movement, spread from culture to culture, was codified, and continues to both inspire and plague the world to this day. Why this one? Somebody has to have expressed some ideas, performed some acts, which captivated enough people so that reports about his life and teachings survived his death and flew from mouth to mouth—forever.

Or not. It doesn't matter.

That is, the existence or not of an historical Jesus makes little difference to many of us who follow him today. He continues to be "real" to us without regard to a grave site, a mound of bones, a tiny fragment of DNA, whatever proof the skeptical mind requires. His reality rests not in historicity but in the truths that reality opens to us about our own nature in relation to the Whole that engulfs it. The beginning of John's glorious but sometimes quite mad portrayal of Jesus, which suggests that Jesus *is* God (and we are not), seems contrary to the truth of Jesus's Incarnation. In Jesus, the Holy meets the human. His life and message reveal not his difference from but his identity with us. He showed us, by being fully human and fully divine, that we too embody divinity and must live our lives so that this reality shines through us and illuminates the world.

This is the wonder of the Resurrection: No matter whether or who Jesus was, how he died, if he rose bodily or in our hearts, he lives!

PART III

CALLED TO ACTION: GOD IN THE WORLD

THE END OF THE WORLD

And those who expected lightning and thunder
Are disappointed.
And those who expected signs and archangels' trumps
Do not believe it is happening now.
As long as the sun and the moon are above,
As long as the bumblebee visits a rose,
As long as rosy infants are born
No one believes it is happening now.

Only a white-haired old man, who would be a prophet
Yet is not a prophet, for he's much too busy,
Repeats while he binds his tomatoes:
There will be no other end of the world,
There will be no other end of the world.

From "A Song on the End of the World,"
CZESLAW MILOSZ, dated Warsaw, 1944

I have been racking my brains, which are the worse for wear after
such rough handling, to think of an appropriate response to the
moral maelstrom that has engulfed humanity since 9/11, an expres-
sion that functions now less as a date than a mark of the-end-of-the-
world-as-we-know-it. If Osama bin Laden intended the attack on the
World Trade Center and terrorist acts before and after it, as George
W. Bush asserted in his September 2001 "Address to a Joint Session
of Congress and the American People," to precipitate the destruction of American customs and practices out of hatred for our free-

doms, he and his fellows have had frightening success. Not that he can be given all the credit. He probably doesn't even know what a full and fair election is, let alone how the complexities of the process in the United States can be exploited so that the winner loses and the loser wins. He's not shipping SUVs into the country or jobs out. I don't know what method of bookkeeping he uses for his vast wealth, but I suspect it's more accurate than U.S. corporate practice. Anything would be.

Sometimes when I tell people that I converted to Catholicism, I add, "So you see, I wasn't born this way; I did this to myself." Analogously, we landed ourselves in most of the messes in which we now flounder long before most of us had even heard of Osama bin Laden and al-Qaeda. The new messes we have created following the attacks on the World Trade Center and the Pentagon dwarf the ones already in place: the murk that arose as the towers collapsed has never entirely cleared and never will. We live differently now, not so much because of the catastrophe—which was horrific beyond all words—but because of the way the events have been exploited to advance the interests and desires of a shockingly small group of people at the expense of the health, in every sense of the word, of humanity. In short, we lost the "war on terrorism" as soon as that phrase was coined, throwing us into a belligerent stance and thus necessitating vast military expenditures at the sacrifice of people's basic human needs for adequate nourishment and shelter, potable water, and air free of deadly contaminants, and I'm not referring to the Iraqi people (or to any other hypothetical "them") here but to U.S. citizens.

Before 9/11, statements like these, which I hope have been construed as critical of our government (indistinguishable now from the megacorporations after which it is increasingly modeled), would have been deemed merely the rantings of left-wing leftover, and so dismissed. Since then, however, some might label them outright treason, and so punishable by incarceration or even death. Now, I don't seriously believe that I'm likely to be carted off for telling you

that I believe that this country is being ruled by a cadre of belligerent and (with notable exceptions) brilliant barons bent on control-
ling the world's resources for their own aggrandizement. I am too
old and too ill to be taken for an enemy of the state. I am simply il-
lustrating the fact that what once seemed unthinkable, the stifling
of free speech, is now routine, as is the constraint of a good many
other liberties.

For those of us who grew up believing, as did the framers of the
Constitution, that no ruler's mandate trumped a basic set of human
rights, this shift really does represent the end of one world and the
beginning of another: darker, more dangerous, perhaps even deadly.
When cartoonist Walt Kelly penned the now famous line "We have
met the enemy and he is us," we could still be amused at the idea.
No longer. "Us" (or U.S.?) too spies on citizens, distorts and withholds information, snatches and tortures prisoners, bombs "the enemy," soldiers and civilians alike, poisons them with radiation and
chemicals, plows them under in mass graves, plunders their resources. Like bullies in a schoolyard, the radical Islamists shout,
"You're the Great Satan and we're going to obliterate you!" Instead
of thinking up ways of changing the rules of engagement or simply
refusing the game altogether, "Us" howls back, "No, *you're* the great
Satan and *we're* going to obliterate *you!*" Trapped in a loop, both
sides dance like perverse dervishes, each waiting for the other to
drop from exhaustion. "Us" uses the terror of terrorists to terrorize
the public into relinquishing the very freedoms "the enemy" is supposed to be trying to take away.

I'm as easily terrified as the next person. When it comes to the fight-
or-flight model of response to menace, you'll definitely catch me
strapping on my running shoes. Appalled by the corruption and
greed I perceive to be the motive forces now driving American society, I just want out of here. Deeply though I love my country (as
distinct from my nation), I want to light out for a place where the

welfare of all children everywhere informs both private and public decisions, where taxation is truly progressive and the moneys collected are spent on programs like universal health care and research into alternative energy sources but not a penny on weapons, where the citizens treat each other and the sojourners among them with civility and tolerance. And if there were such a place, I'd probably have my airline ticket in hand. Actually, I wouldn't still be here, rattling on at you. I'd be off in utopia.

So making a dash for it isn't a feasible response even if it were an appropriate one. And I don't believe that it is. Nor is its opposite in the classic stress model, standing my ground, baring my teeth, pouncing on my enemy and tearing him to pieces (unless he shreds me first). In so doing, I would be acting in the very way that my enemy has acted toward me. How am I going to affirm the life that the terrorists seek to obliterate and counter the death-dealing methods adopted by people in power in response to their hatred if I adopt the same destructive tactics? I'd be no more effective than the foolish tigers in the children's story who chased each other around the base of a tree until, in the hot sun, they melted into ghee.

The fight-or-flight model was based on studies of male subjects, as the preponderance of all research has been until recently. A study at UCLA, focusing on female responses to distress, uncovered quite a different and much more social pattern, which the investigators termed "tend and befriend." Oxytocin, generated by both males and females under duress, is enhanced by estrogen but inhibited by male hormones. Perhaps as a result of these differing hormonal responses to oxytocin, women tend to cope by nurturing their children or seeking out others, friends or even strangers, for support.[1] Withdrawal and aggression, it would appear, are not universal responses, as we've been led to believe. Such a study demonstrates that other models, even at the biological level, can exist. The moral implications of this diversity cry out to be envisioned and explored.

I would call the model I'm about to sketch a Christian response if the label "Christian" didn't suggest so many beliefs I don't hold. As I use it, I intend it to mean faithful to the fundamental teachings of Jesus. Even he is a hypothetical creation, of course, not just because his historical existence can only be posited, not proved, but because his original being has, in the course of centuries, been so thickly overlaid with invention that it can no longer be discerned, any more than one can see the precipitating grain of sand when gazing at a pearl. In this sense, any way one speaks of him, whether as Christos or simply as Jesus, can only ever be an imaginative construct. As my husband has often said, when you talk about Jesus, you reveal little—maybe nothing—about Jesus but a great deal about yourself. I don't claim that anything I say to you about him is Truer than anything a great many others have said, although I speak from a more radical locus than most. (I adopt the word "radical" not in the political and largely pejorative sense to which it has been reduced but in the sense of its origin in the Latin word *radix*, root.) I am trying to come at the essential ideas that set Christianity in motion and to conceive a world based on their implementation.

This will take the form of a thought experiment based on the premise of the Good News: The Kindom of God exists right here, right now, among us. *What?* we are likely to squawk, looking at the mess around us. *Where?* I am reminded of my daughter's reaction when, right after her college graduation, I took her to New York City. After a night in the old Algonquin Hotel, we walked over to the old Times Square. She stared in one direction and another. "You mean," she said at last in a small voice, "this is *it?*" I realized that she had never seen it except on television, thronged with revelers waiting for the ball to drop on New Year's Eve. Similarly, we have fantastic images of God's Kindom, shaped by centuries of literary imagination and convention: the land without sorrow or sighing, flowing with milk and honey, where even the beasts cuddle up together and nobody has to do anything more taxing than cast down his golden crown at the edge of the glassy sea, a place ever-promised, not yet entered, but soon... but soon...

Jesus is not making a promise here. He's stating a reality: the Kindom of God is in our midst, whether we can perceive it or not. We may dwell in it; we may not; or (and I think this is the most likely scenario) we may drift in and out of it depending on our current level of consciousness. Jesus's teachings provide a way (although I'm not sure he would claim it the only way) to achieve and sustain it. What I'm wondering is how the world might be altered if we responded to its vagaries according to his basic precepts: tranquility, forgiveness, generosity, love. These are "warm fuzzy" words, easily acknowledged and then dismissed in the face of the myriad practical concerns that dominate our lives. But Jesus means them not as ideals (wouldn't it be great if we all loved each other) but as practices (you must love everyone you encounter, and believe me, some of them are going to be pretty smelly or scary). *Okay*, we say, taking a deep breath. *We understand. Tell us what to do.*

Be calm and trust in God's goodness.

Peace does not begin with the establishment and maintenance of an impressive military force, or the manufacture of high-tech weapons that threaten an opponent's annihilation. It does not begin with the deployment of personnel and their use of these weapons against people whom most of them will never see. It does not even begin with the signing of a treaty. It begins in the heart that rejects fear and affirms its own value in the vast Unfoldment of which it is a minute yet significant part.

"What do sparrows cost?" Jesus asks "A dime a dozen? Yet not one of them is overlooked by God... Don't be so timid: You're worth more than a flock of sparrows" (Luke 12:6–7). Most of us are as easily spooked as sparrows, and overcoming timidity doesn't come naturally. It requires preparation and practice. In one study, the brain of a meditating Tibetan Buddhist monk didn't register startlement even when a sound like a gunshot went off by his head.[2] The average person isn't likely to spend years in deep meditation. Nevertheless, we can choose to alter our behavior in ways that foster feelings of tranquility and trust.

For a start, we could stop using the word "terrorist," which places in the hands of others the power to paralyze us with fear. This fear has suited the purposes of a band of angry men made dangerous by their hatred of an invention, "the West," which they perceive to threaten their cherished beliefs. In other words, they themselves are operating out of fear, the foundations of which are so nonrational that we may be able to do very little to allay it. But terror has also suited the purposes of many in our own government, who play on it to drum up support for acts that might be resisted by a confident population. If they scare us enough with their rhetoric of intimidation, we're likely to put ourselves under their protection and do whatever they tell us will ensure our safety, which alas seems to involve performing murderous acts that will further arouse the hatred and fear of "terrorists."

As a writer, I devote a good deal of energy to recognizing and eliminating clichés, those clusters of words that fall trippingly from our tongues without first making a trip through our brains. Sometimes the effect on both speaker and listener is trivial: how much does it matter that you can, of course, have your cake and eat it too; what you can't do is eat your cake and have it too. But some instances are outright dangerous, and we've been menaced by one of these for years: "the war on terror." Everybody uses the phrase. When somebody abuses it, as vice presidential candidate Dick Cheney did during the 2004 presidential campaign in suggesting that unless you voted for him and George W. Bush, you were inviting countrywide devastation, there was plenty of outcry at his scare tactics, but I didn't see anyone question his underlying premise or the words he used to encode it: the war on terror, the war on terror, the war on terror. In fact, they simply echoed it without stopping to analyze its meaning. That's how I make my living: tunneling into language and extracting flecks of significance.

Apparently, we don't even use the correct word to designate the actions of our opponents. We speak of *jihad*, translating it as *holy war*, when to mainstream Muslims it signifies a spiritual struggle. "The Qur'an refers to *jihad* only in terms of intellectual effort to apply divine revelation in promoting peace through justice," writes Islamist scholar Robert D. Crane. The appropriate term is *hirabah*, which refers to "public terrorism in a war against society and civilization. In legal terminology it is defined as 'spreading mischief in the land,' but its precise meaning, as defined by Professor Khalid Abou el Fadl, is 'killing by stealth and targeting a defenseless victim in a way intended to cause terror in society.' This is the Islamic definition of terrorism. It is the very opposite of *jihad*."[3] If we sorted the words out, Anisa Mehdi asserts, "think of the disincentive to young, hungry, cynical Muslims—angry at their own governments and angry at ours for bolstering theirs. If they heard 'hirabah' instead of 'jihad,' if they heard 'murder' instead of 'martyr,' if they heard they were bound for hell instead of heaven, they might not be so quick to sign up to kill themselves and a handful of so-called 'infidels' along with them."[4]

Now let's stop to ponder "terror"—a state of intense fear—and "terrorist"—the one who throws you into that state. Is that really what we want to say, that we now live in dread and that a bunch of malevolent strangers have put us and kept us there? In doing so, don't we give them the power to determine the tenor and even the details of our lives, eliciting Orwellian behaviors like spying on the general populace, intimidating "deviants" from a state-imposed politico-religious standard, imprisoning and torturing people without habeas corpus, militarizing our borders, corrupting our language so that war is peace, freedom is slavery, ignorance is strength?

Haven't the attackers in this way got what they want: our ruination? I am not willing to accede to them. Nor am I willing to conduct a "war" on them. As a radical pacifist, I reject war on principle, but especially in this context. It's too narrow and rigid a response, in a situation in which we need, perhaps more than we ever have before, the full range of human attitudes and actions at our disposal.

I don't mean to suggest, in rejecting "the war on terror," that I dismiss or take lightly the seriousness of the situation in which we have found ourselves since 9/11 (and indeed, for those with any historical sense, well before then). On the contrary, I resent the ease with which people repeat the phrase and the knee-jerk responses it elicits. No one is paying enough attention. I believe with George Orwell that "if thought corrupts language, language can also corrupt thought." To avoid debasing ourselves, I want us to think about every single sound we make, to choose very carefully the words with which we express it, and to listen closely and critically to both our own utterances and those of others.

I don't have a single catchphrase like "the war on terror" to suggest. In fact, I don't want to suggest any particular phrase. I want you to choose your own, as I have been doing. My choice has varied through time and reflection, but I always try to be as precise as possible. Since I'm not scared, no matter what color the terror chart is turned, I call our attackers a variety of names, among them "madmen" and "mean-sons-of-bitches." More seriously, I think of them as mass murderers. And my response to them is defiant rather than bellicose. Why restrict yourself to the tactics of war when you have so many other resources at hand?

The politicians don't want us to reflect like this, patiently and flexibly, on what they are saying. From their point of view, terror is the ideal state for the electorate, who will flock to them for protection. (Ask yourself, what kind of creature "flocks"?) Molly Ivins quoted George Gerbner in this regard: "Fearful people are more dependent, more easily manipulated and controlled, more susceptible to deceptively simple, strong, tough measures and hard-line postures... They may accept and even welcome repression if it promises to relieve their insecurities."[5] If we want to make any progress toward peace, we must refuse scare tactics whoever is employing them. We might call the "terrorists" something that doesn't reduce us to quaking children but permits us to confront them as equals. Why not use the name they have given themselves, al-Qaeda, and refer to ourselves as the United States, even if they do call us the Great Satan. We know who we are.

Or do we?

Judge and correct yourself, not others.

Self-scrutiny has never ranked very high on any list of American virtues I've come across. We're apt to dismiss it as navel-gazing or scab-picking and move on to some more practical (and preferably profitable) activity. We're quick enough to condemn the behavior of others, say, possessing weapons of mass destruction, but fail to note anything peculiar about permitting the same[6] to ourselves. "Why do you notice the sliver in your friend's eye, but overlook the timber in your own?" Jesus asks. "How can you say to your friend, 'Friend, let me get the sliver in your eye,' when you do not notice the timber in your own? You phony, first take the timber out of your own eye, and then you'll see well enough to remove the sliver in your friend's eye" (Luke 6:40–42). *Oh, but it's different for us*, we hasten to object. *We need these weapons to ensure the safety of the whole world, because we're strong and wise, unlike those crazy little men over there, who are determined to destroy us all in a nuclear holocaust or a ravage of smallpox or something that we would never do (never mind the incinerated Japanese or the infected Indians, that was different)*. Despite all our protestations, though, it wasn't different, still isn't different, will never be different. The crazy little men are not necessarily over there. When we read that we had to stop the leader who "has pursued his ambition to dominate Iraq and the broader Middle East using the only means he knows, intimidation, coercion and annihilation of all those who might stand in his way,"[7] we have to stop and think which of several leaders Colin Powell might have been describing. As long as any possess weapons of mass destruction, all put the world in mortal danger.

"The standard you apply will be the standard applied to you," Jesus warns (Luke 6:38). Even as we mourn the three thousand who died in the events of 9/11, we must acknowledge that on that day and every day since, twenty-five thousand people have died of hunger or hunger-related causes,[8] brought on not only by drought, floods, and disease but also by the policies of governments and corporations (if the two can any longer be distinguished) that encourage deforestation, land erosion, the abandonment of subsistence farming for cash crops like coffee and cocaine, and so on, frequently leading to political turmoil that results in repressive regimes, many of them hospitable to the aforementioned governments and corporations. Once again the tigers chase each other around the palm tree, only this time the substance they melt into is not clarified butter but bitter poison. That the three thousand died because of furious religious hatred and the starving because of greed for resources and power makes no difference. Dead people are still dead, no matter how they got that way. God grieves the loss of every one of them.

Respond to wrongs not with retaliation but with disproportionate generosity.

There is more than enough culpability to go around. But neither blame nor hand-wringing serve to alter the world in ways that might promote its survival. We must behave toward one another altogether differently than we might have done in earlier times when, although enemies might slaughter each other's troops wholesale, the mayhem was confined to a specific and generally quite limited geographical area: Hastings, Agincourt, Gallipoli, Antietam. One of the consequences of the globalization that developed during the last century and continues apace in this one is that all the world's a battlefield and all the men and women merely potential casualties. All. We really can eradicate all life (except maybe the cockroaches) at will. We may already be doing so.

Instead of retaliation, which seems to come to us naturally, we must learn reconciliation, which apparently does not (but only apparently—keep in mind "tend and befriend"). What if, rather than "getting even," which always implies returning harm for harm, we adopted an altogether different economy, based upon Jesus's injunction to give without expecting anything in return, and not just to give but give more than is called for. "When someone strikes you on the cheek, offer the other as well," Jesus instructs. "When someone takes away your coat, don't prevent that person from taking your shirt along with it" (Luke 6:29).

I doubt that he literally intends us to run around bruised and naked, but from these concrete examples we get the message: Do the utterly unexpected by being not reactive to another's wrongdoing but proactive in your own largesse. Similarly the Buddha teaches: "Never retaliate in kind. Hatred does not come to an end through hatred but can only cease through generosity." Imagine how we could confound our enemies if we were to leap out of the deadly pas de deux (or trois or quatre) of warfare and begin some different dance, new rhythms, new gestures, leaving our would-be opponents with gaping mouths or empty arms.

Let's say, for example, that we had taken the $300+ billion the Iraq war cost as of 2006 and spent it on food, medicines, infrastructure, and environmental cleanup for the Iraqi people. What could Saddam Hussein ever have done to top that? Although I'm no economist, I'm guessing we'd have enough left over to take care of other problems, like our own crumbling infrastructure and shambles of a medical system. If we're going to spend the money anyway, why not get some measurable return on our investment: linear feet of bridges built or restored, numbers of vials of vaccine exhausted in inoculating children against measles, quantity of surplus grain taken out of stockpiles and distributed wherever malnourishment threatens infant brain development.

If forbearance and generosity were sufficient, at least some of us might succeed in behaving well. But Jesus commands, and this lies at the very heart of the Gospel message, that we go even further: "Love your enemies." He isn't talking about some warm upwelling in the heart, which comes readily enough in a reciprocal relationship. He isn't referring to an emotional state at all. He is imposing a discipline, the most strenuous one imaginable: to regard people who bear the utmost hostility toward us and treat us in the vilest ways as our fellow human beings, worthy of God's love and therefore of ours. He does not ask us to validate their feelings or approve their actions but to work at embracing such people in spite of these. It's an idea of astonishing simplicity and beauty, and I'd like to assure you that it can be carried out, but I'm not sure I've ever managed it. Love Osama bin Laden after what he ordered done to a host of innocents on a bright autumn morning? Love Kim Jong Il, who allows the North Korean people to starve while military expenditures consume nearly a third of the GDP? Love George W. Bush, ranting about the right to life of the unborn child whilst employing "shock and awe" tactics against millions of born ones (half the population of Iraq is under fifteen)? Yes. Yes. Yes. I don't know how, but God does it, and expects no less from us. If we concentrated fully on loving our enemies, we'd have neither the energy nor the inclination left over for killing.

Oh come on, Nancy, I can guess you're thinking about now. Get real. The hell you don't believe in will freeze over before Donald Rumsfeld and his like practice loving the wretches imprisoned in Guantánamo and Abu Ghraib—or they, him. Hatred and fear fuel the human response to a menacing stranger, and war is the natural consequence. You're never going to reassure the majority of people sufficiently so that they don't stampede to war whenever their leaders shout that the sky is falling and the only way to keep it in place is to drop bombs out of it. Even if you could, you're never going to persuade those leaders to engage in activities that will undermine their own perpetuation. They will do anything, even subvert the electoral process, to get and keep power. And you forgot about the oil. No businessman, smart or dim, is going to pass up the opportunity to wrest control of 300 billion barrels of oil and 110 trillion cubic feet of natural gas. Never mind what Jesus would say, do, or drive. Think of the profits!

I know all that. I'm not *stupid*. I just don't care. If we all sat around waiting for the other guy to see the light, we'd be squatting here in the darkness for the rest of our days. My task—and yours— as I see it is to *be* the light. Incandescence takes a lot of energy. Who can waste any looking around to count how many other people are switching on? If I believe in values like trust, personal rectitude, generosity, forgiveness, and love, I must practice them whether or not anyone else is doing so (and millions upon millions *are* doing so). Virtue is proactive, not reactive, and the majority doesn't rule. Nevertheless, the more the merrier.

Enough of us, and we could create an utterly new world: not the world as we have known it, safe and comfortable for us but bearing, in its inequities, the seeds of its own destruction; not the one that has taken its place, in which fear and hostility have been created and then inflamed to serve the several agendas of men who lust after power or wealth or salvation or various bizarre combinations of the three; but a third world with a fresh set of characteristics (one of which would be the absence of the old world's Third World). Even in the realm of science, paradigm shifts are rare, rarer still when it comes to human behavior. But a well-developed paradigm for our third world exists already, eclipsed but not extinguished by the testosterone-driven worldview of those who, for some centuries, have arrogated the power of defining large-scale human interactions to themselves. Throughout that time, half the world has been biochemically predisposed to an irenic alternative of sustenance and intimacy: a model that reflects remarkably well the teachings of Jesus before they fell into the hands of the patristic fathers. Since it is intrinsically affiliative rather than combative, I'm darned if I can see how it can be made into the "dominant" mode of human interaction. But I think that it's got to prevail if we want any human beings left to interact. We may not have a lot of time. I suggest we get to work.

WHERE GOD LIVES

What if God's unknowability is the most illuminating profundity humans can know about God? That would mean that religious language, instead of opening into the absolute certitude on which all forms of triumphal superiority are based, would open into true modesty. The closed creation, in which every question has an answer, would be replaced by an infinite cosmos where every answer sparks a new question. If what we mean by "God" is the living pulse of such open-endedness, then God is of no use in systems of dominance, censorship, power. God is everywhere, yes. But, also, God is nowhere.

JAMES CARROLL

I am not especially sanguine about humanity's prospects. If there ever was a time when we could have turned down some less agonistic route, could have elected to balance our desires with our needs and the needs of the rest of creation, that time has passed. And maybe there never was such a time, except in dreams. God only knows. At any rate, our technological capabilities have now so far outstripped our moral development that it seems likely that we really will (and sooner rather than later) blow ourselves up with nuclear devices or suffocate ourselves with petrol fumes or poison ourselves with chemical waste or drown ourselves in melted ice. There's no reason—apart from our own egocentricity—to think that the human species is going to survive over the long term or to view our extinction as an outrage. God loves us boundlessly but not best. The cosmos is infinite, and events will keep unfolding forever. One of them might be a minute flare toward the edge of a small galaxy signaling our passage.

"But if you believe that we may be approaching the end," a friend asks, "how can you keep up your activism? Why don't you just give up?" It's a valid question, I suppose. Most people act out of a belief that what they do will make a difference, at least on a personal scale; and social activists tend to believe that they can effect not just systemic change but actual improvement.

"I guess I'm just cussed," I reply. "I'm damned if I'm going to let my behavior be shaped by warmongers and death-dealers. As long as I resist them, I bear witness to another way of being in the world."

I do not doubt the existence, in the here and now, of the condition variously referred to as the Kingdom of God, the reign of God, God's imperial rule, or more recently, the Kindom of God. When I first heard this final phrase, I dismissed it as too cute and touchy-feely to be used seriously, but it's grown on me over time. It shifts the emphasis from God's domination over us to God's relationship with us and ours with one another. If God is, among the many things God is, Abba (and Amma) for us all, then we are spiritual siblings as surely as mitochondrial DNA shows us to be biological ones. In which case, we would do well to stop behaving like a dysfunctional family and find ways to strengthen one another.

I'm not suggesting that we strive toward that persistent and pernicious myth, "one big happy family." In fact, I think that's where we keep going wrong. We hold out for some *Life with Father* scenario, which God is going to produce for us in some far future if only we're good enough. (The baddies will get tossed into a fiery furnace. Unless all of us burn ourselves up in a fiery furnace of our own device, of course.) While we're holding out for perfection, we hold ourselves back from the work required to establish and enter the state of which Jesus says in the Gnostic Gospel of Thomas, "It will not come by watching for it. It will not be said, 'Look, here!' or 'Look there!' Rather, the Father's imperial rule is spread out upon the earth, and people don't see it" (Thom. 113:2–4). It's here all right. The trick is *discernment.*

You can enter it at will, any time, wherever you are. The key word is "will." It's not like a house with open doors or a city with open gates, which you have only to occupy. It's more like the hammer and nails, the stones and mortar from which these can be constructed. It's a project. It's *work.* A few people have a lot of stamina and can keep at it without cease. I think of Mother Teresa. Like most, I manage it only fitfully, though more often and for longer periods as I practice. I concentrate on the simplest of rules, codified traditionally as the seven corporal works of mercy:

- to feed the hungry;
- to give drink to the thirsty;
- to clothe the naked;
- to visit and ransom the captives;
- to shelter the homeless;
- to visit the sick;
- to bury the dead.

One is supposed to perform these acts in order to secure the eternal salvation of one's soul. Personally, I'm not concerned about my salvation. My salvation is a question to be settled at another time. I'm concerned about the sheer bodily salvation of humanity. But since I am unable to grasp, either physically or intellectually, the whole of humanity, I have to go about it one person at a time.

Here are a few places I go where I know God lives:

Su Casa The gate is always locked, because some of the residents wander. One of them, a sweet-faced woman wearing several layers of clothing, hovers near as a worker turns her key to let George and me in.

"Are you going to take me with you?" the woman asks. I can't tell whether she's hopeful or apprehensive.

"No," I tell her. "I've come to visit." She remains by the gate as I wheel onto the patio. A man with flyaway white hair and bulging blue eyes thrusts himself into my path and grasps my hand.

"I'm sorry for your trouble," he says, glancing at my wheelchair and then staring into my eyes. "I will pray for you."

"Thank you. I will pray for you too."

"Peace be with you."

"And also with you," I reply, extricating my hand from his light but persistent grasp and turning so as not to run over his toes. I head down the slope, past a large bed of jonquils, to the building where Sharon lives. There are four units in this complex. Su Casa itself is a nursing home; the others provide assisted living. George heads for one, I for another. When I sought to volunteer as a nursing-home visitor under the sponsorship of Love Thy Neighbor Ministries in Tucson, the director inquired whether I had accepted Jesus Christ as my personal savior and was plainly troubled when I replied that I had not, because doing so would require me to believe in damnation, a fate God loves us far too much to impose. He read me several passages from Scripture, and admonished me how urgent it was that we bring the people we work with to Jesus Christ, even on their deathbeds, for the sake of their immortal souls, but he didn't make this belief a condition for taking me on. So now I visit Sharon, who also has MS. Born a Mormon, she's now a Buddhist, insofar as she embraces any tradition, and I'm far more concerned that her bottom be kept free of bedsores than her soul unblemished by sin.

When I go into her unit, the television is playing to a living room empty but for a puff of smoky fur named Silverbell, who is not watching. Sharon's room is at the end of a narrow hallway. I tap and then push open the door. She has been sleeping, and I apologize for waking her, but she quickly rolls over and works her way into her wheelchair, chattering eagerly. Although her speech is severely slurred, she appears to be cognitively intact. Since most of the residents plainly are not, she doesn't get much conversation except with the workers, when they can spare the time, and with me for an hour on Tuesday afternoons. She has four sons, but they live in other states and refuse to visit, she says, for fear of catching her disease. Her sister comes from Alaska about once a year.

"I gotta have a cigarette," she says, calling an aide to push her. A power chair would make life easier for both her and the staff. I wonder whether I should look into how she could get one. I don't want to be pushy. We wheel back up to the patio, where another aide circulates like a cigarette girl in an old film, but dumpier, doling out cigarettes and lighting them on demand. Everyone here seems to smoke, and the air under the covered porch is rank. This seems odd in a health facility, but the staff may figure that these people have little enough pleasure in their lives—and anyway, several of them light up too.

George has returned to the patio with Tim, a man in his forties, once a construction worker with a wife and children. The damage caused by surgery for a brain aneurysm has skewed his social judgment, and he tends to act toward me like a teasing adolescent, blocking my wheelchair with his large, soft body, asking me what George has got that he hasn't. Having found out that Tim loves jokes, George has brought a sheaf of them from the Internet, and Tim happily regales us with faintly off-color humor.

After about an hour, we say our goodbyes. One day I will probably live in a place like this, but for now, by the grace of George, I can still wheel out the gate and across the street to our van and so home to our pretty little house.

"Thanks for coming," Sharon says when I leave.

"Thanks for letting me visit," I reply. I mean it. I don't think I'm very good at this. Reclusive by inclination, I have to force myself out of that pretty little house every week. Maybe Sharon feels the same way about me. *Oh groan, here comes that dumb volunteer again, and I'll have to be nice to her for a whole hour.* But after Sharon has spent an hour with me, my spirits lift. My reclusion then strikes me as self-indulgent, the habit developed by a woman with a long history of agoraphobia in order to deflect the discomfort she feels in social settings. Personal ease has no particular value for the work of affirming God's presence in the world. I can't think of a single instance in the Gospels when Jesus says to his followers, "Make yourselves comfortable." On the contrary.

SMU II The road leading from Tucson to the Arizona State Prison Complex in Florence slices across hot open desert, and at a distance the buildings and watchtowers shimmer like a mirage. By the time you turn off the highway onto Butte Avenue, they have solidified, squatting in clusters—East Unit, CB6, Cook, Rynning, the Special Management Units, I and II—each grimmer than the last. At SMU II you run out of road. You have reached, in every way, the end of the line. The structure is a windowless dark gray concrete bunker, surrounded by two twenty-foot fences topped with giant loops of razor wire. You can't just walk into this place. Or, needless to say, out. Until the last twenty-four to forty-eight hours, when an inmate is moved to the Death House.

Each time George and I come up here, we approach reluctantly. We've grabbed lunch at Burger King, the only nearby eatery, but even the unaccustomed Whopper and fries doesn't account for the churning in our stomachs. We've stopped at the prison store, which sells clothing, art, and jewelry produced by the prisoners. Except for the men on death row, who are no longer allowed to possess any materials with which they might fashion anything. One, I know, painstakingly unravels his socks and weaves the fibers into crosses, which he smuggles to a woman who sells them, giving him a tiny and erratic income; George wears one under his clothing until the threads give way and he has to put on a new one. Sometimes at the store we buy flannel-lined denim jackets, crudely made but warm, for the homeless people who eat at Our Lady of Guadalupe Chapel and Free Kitchen.

We've driven through the guarded gate, stopping to show our IDs, and wound past one unit after another until we pulled into this enormous and nearly empty asphalt parking lot. We've stripped my wheelchair of the nylon pouches I use in lieu of a briefcase or backpack. George has removed his car key from the ring and tossed the rest of his keys under the seat. Now it's two o'clock. Time to go in.

"We're here to see Eric King," we say to the guard (they call themselves officers), handing over our IDs and receiving badges in return. George steps through a metal detector as another guard wands me, and we join a silent little cluster by the rear door. I'm forever breaking the dress code. The first time I came, I wore a peach-colored silk blouse and was told it was too close to the international orange worn by the prisoners. I also had a string of carved bears around my neck, and all jewelry is forbidden except for earrings and religious symbols. Fortunately, the young female guard, perhaps sensing that I was a novice, declared that my blouse wasn't *really* orange and that bears, because they are sacred to many Native peoples, were acceptable. Another time, a different guard wasn't so indulgent. Because I was wearing a sleeveless top, also forbidden (I hadn't read the dress code in a while), I would have to stay behind. We had nothing in the car but an old rubber-backed rug, so I spent two sweltering hours with that wrapped around my naked shoulders. The purpose of such restrictions is to prevent gang paraphernalia or provocative dress, of course, but you'd think that few people would mistake me for a chola or a tart.

When we've all been screened, the door in front of us unlocks and a guard escorts us into the space between the fences; the next door doesn't unlock until the one behind us clicks. We troop across a yard defoliated of even a stray desert weed, true scorched earth, and into a vestibule leading to the two visitation rooms. These are dim spaces lined with glass cubicles, each faced by two plastic chairs, and a guard at a desk in the center.

"There he is!" I say, peering swiftly from window to window until I make out Eric's dark face smiling at us. "I need a hug," he said to me in one of his letters, and I long to throw my arms around him, but death row inmates are never permitted contact visits, not even a farewell embrace before being led to execution. We touch palms through the thick glass and begin to chat. Even though a sensitive microphone conveys our voices, George, normally soft-spoken, tends to shout, as though sheer volume could break down the barriers—not just physical but educational, economic, experiential—between us.

Eric is a large, soft, forty-year-old with terrible teeth. "I am always hungry," he often writes, and although he complains about the food, he eats it, I'm sure, attempting to fill his emptiness. I'm afraid he spends the small money orders we send from time to time on sweets from the prison store. He refuses to exercise, either in his cell or in the small high-walled area to which he could go, alone, for an hour three times a week. He cannot see but can hear the inmates around him, but he refuses to converse with them. He has a television, and once in a while he attempts to read. Months go by between visits from us or from his elderly mother; those of his ten siblings who aren't also incarcerated refuse to come.

As a consequence of his isolation, his conversational skills are rusty. At first, we couldn't make it through the full two hours allotted because the antipsychotic medication he was taking made him so drowsy that his words would trail off and his eyelids droop, but more recently he's been refusing the drugs. The voices haven't come back, he reports, and we find him definitely more alert. We're even surprised when the guard notifies us that the visit must end. As we "hold hands," George says a prayer of thanksgiving for our friendship. Wrung out, George and I plunge into the desert glare. Probably equally wrung out, Eric will be led, in shackles, back to the eight-by-ten-foot space that will be his only "house" until he dies. Letters will pass between us, but months will go by before we steel ourselves for another drive up Highway 79.

Nothing in my religious upbringing prepared me for finding God in a man wearing an orange jumpsuit and locked in a wire cage, grinning in pure delight at the sight of me. Immortal, invisible, and wise, God was wholly removed from humanity, a stern and judgmental Parent whom we all-but-vainly prayed to please. Whatever an "incarnate Word" might have been, it certainly didn't have anything to do with bodies. Coming to believe, as experience and reflection have taught me to do, that each of us is responsible for bearing God into the world, I must accept that this task falls to Eric every bit as much as it falls to me. Not that Eric *is* God, any more than you or I are. But we each provide a means for God to manifest Godself to our dull senses.

This point throws me against a conundrum I have never resolved: the capacity of God-bearers to think and act in ways one can only describe as ungodly. I harbor no illusions about Eric, who has spent well over half his life in prison, convicted of assault and murder. During the seven years he served for the former offense, he might well have been rehabilitated, but he was given neither education nor social training; and only a few months after his release, while high on alcohol and cocaine, he shot dead a convenience store clerk and a security guard in the course of a robbery. Opposing capital punishment because it vitiates the social soul, I don't believe that he should be executed, but he is now in no condition ever to be released. The course of his life can be explained but never excused; as the mother of a murdered child, I know too well the pain he is capable of inflicting. Even so, mysteriously, his essential value is unimpaired. I don't understand this. I only know it.

Even here, God lives.

The Corner of Speedway and Euclid On Fridays I dress in black, sit on a street corner, and smile at the occupants of every car that drives by, practicing what may be the world's truly oldest profession: peacemaking. After all, so far we're still here, aren't we, no thanks to the guys wielding everything from rocks and clubs through maces and long bows and muskets to bombs that are smarter than they are. We've been standing here from time immemorial. We'll never "win" against them. For us, human experience is not constructed around victory and defeat. We simply are. And through our being, we affirm the possibility of looking at the world in another way.

Every week since August 2001, at five o'clock on Friday afternoons, a group calling themselves Women in Black gathers in front of the First Christian Church at one of Tucson's busiest intersections. Modeled after vigils that were started in Israel in 1988 and have since spread around the globe, the group was formed by a handful of activists to protest against Israel's occupation of the West Bank and Gaza. After the events of the following month, the focus broadened to a plea for peace everywhere. In the early days, perhaps only ten or a dozen people showed up. Now we get as many as a hundred.

You don't have to wear black to attend our vigil. You don't even have to be a woman. Although many of us engage in religious practices—offhand, I can think of Catholics, Jews, Friends, Unitarian Universalists, Muslims, Presbyterians, and Congregationalists—the only commitment required is to nonviolence. This diversity reflects an important point about God's Kindom that tends to be ignored: the kindom comes about not because people espouse a prescribed set of principles (too often thought of by their believers as the One True Faith), adherence to which will produce a desired result (generally involving the salvation of some but by no means all of creation), but because they behave in ways that enable all creation to thrive. God draws no distinctions among the multitudinous stripes of Christianity, Buddhism, secular humanism, or Jainism (though if I were God I might confess a secret weakness for the Jains). God appears whenever any of these use their beliefs to guide themselves toward such behavior. We stand well back from the street, leaving the sidewalk clear for pedestrians. Some situations call for civil disobedience, but this is not one of them. Those who prefer a silent vigil stand along Speedway, the chatterers stand along Euclid. I prefer silence, although the sun drives me around the corner in the summer. Even there, I try to stay out of conversations. This is the one hour in my week in which to focus my whole attention on peace. The people around me hold up signs and banners. Because my weak hands can't hold anything, I have fashioned a sign out of thick poster board that can be hung on a lanyard around my neck, black letters glued to a white ground: WE ARE ONE. I repeat this silently as a mantra, trying to look at individual motorists as I do, to smile at them, to remind and reassure them that even though the government is determined at all costs (and God knows how high these will turn out to be) to wage war, theirs is only a choice, not an inevitability. Some of us will act otherwise.

I wish I had not had to engage in this activity virtually without respite for nearly forty years. When I began, I may really have believed that I could help to put an end to war. Now I know otherwise. Yet here I am, a witness to human folly. From the cacophony of horns and the peace signs waved through car windows, I know that many others at least oppose the nation's current campaigns even if they don't share my radical pacifism. For one reason or another, they can't come out here. I can. So I do. Every so often voices, almost invariably young and male, shout "Fuck you!" or "War! War!" and twice we even got mooned. It has occurred to me, in a world where firearms proliferate, that one of us might get shot.

I really do believe that we are one, transitory coalescences of stellar stuff that will in time dissipate, our infinitesimal particles scattering and reforming in the endless reel that constitutes the cosmos, resurrection upon resurrection upon resurrection. In this iteration, the agglomeration of particles chanced to form an entity with the capacity for consciousness, and so I am an "I." I'm awfully glad I happened, even if only for a while, but one of the consequences of consciousness is a sense of separation from "people" and "objects." I can intuit that these "others" do not represent reality, but I cannot experience oneness. I practice as I sit here, grit coating my teeth, fumes stinging my eyes. I don't think I'll ever achieve the state called for by Thich Nhat Hanh in *The Miracle of Mindfulness*:

> Feelings, whether of compassion or irritation, should be welcomed, recognized, and treated on an absolutely equal basis; because both are ourselves. The tangerine I am eating is me. The mustard greens I am planting are me. I plant with all my heart and mind. I clean this teapot with the kind of attention I would have were I giving the baby Buddha or Jesus a bath. Nothing should be treated more carefully than anything else. In mindfulness, compassion, irritation, mustard green plant, and teapot are all sacred.

But I have learned this: God is here.

I have laid out these examples of my own work and witness in order to demonstrate a couple of points. For one thing, the entrance to the kindom is neither hidden nor barred. Those who teach otherwise are trying to mystify the way for a variety of reasons, most of them not very admirable. The truth is that if large numbers of perfectly ordinary people began to take care of each other and the creation in which we are all embedded, a lot of people who trade in human misery would lose their access to wealth and supremacy (which are not elements of the kindom). The reality is that most people are unlikely ever to do so. That's no excuse for inaction.

I place emphasis on "ordinary." The fact that a few individuals in every age have been exceptionally proficient at performing works of mercy (think of Dorothy Day) or at witnessing to human wrongs and calling for their correction (think of Martin Luther King Jr.) does not mean that these require superhuman skills. Even the least among us can perform small and often pedestrian acts of good-will: buying disposable diapers for a mother who can't afford them; spreading peanut butter on day-old bread at the soup kitchen; reading stories to preschoolers at the library; scooping up the poop of other people's dogs; telephoning your representatives, the president, and your elderly mother. Smiling. It's very difficult to harbor hatred and fear with the corners of your mouth turned up. Try it. No, not a grimace like that. Soften your facial muscles, curve your lips, squint your eyes a little. Don't wait until you have something to smile about, because you might have to wait a good long time. Just do it.

To the greatest extent you can, take care of the wider world as well. The works of mercy Catholicism enjoins may take place one at a time, but taken together they gain considerable force. We can all serve one another and collectively conserve the earth's abundance. George and I have been able to buy a small, thick-walled house with solar hot water, photovoltaic cells for generating electricity, and Xeriscaping, so as to conserve natural resources. We have friends who have traded their gas-guzzlers for hybrids. (Unfortunately, a hybrid wheelchair-accessible van hasn't yet been engineered, so we're still slurping away.) One principled couple we know buys only goods made in the USA, refusing to participate in the exploitation of poor laborers around the globe. Buy your clothing from secondhand stores and your produce from local growers. Go on a shopping spree at a thrift store or supermarket (changing the world should be fun) and drop off your booty at a homeless shelter. If you employ any workers, make sure you pay them whatever the living (not the minimum) wage is in your area. With any luck, some people will follow your example. Many more will not. Don't worry. You can pray for but you cannot effect conversion in others. Attend to your own.

My other point is that the kindom, insofar as we can enter it, is not a place or a space or a state of perfect ease. It is not awarded as a trophy for obeying the rules. It offers neither voluptuous maidens nor celestial gardens nor angelic strains plucked on golden harps. Rather, it is a process, and not necessarily a pleasurable one. It is what you do, not where you are. In fact, if you find yourself thoroughly comfortable, you have probably veered away from it into a complacent or distracted condition, which, though not intrinsically bad, is beside the point. And to tell the truth, you don't have all the time in the world. Why waste any more of it than you have to (and the frailty of human nature dictates that we will always fill up our hours and our spirits with spiritual rubbish unless we pay more attention to good housekeeping than most of us generally do). Don't wait! Wake up! Listen! The more often you practice the kindom, the more aware you become that the Holy is present. In pain. In sorrow. In terror. In delight. Even though you will die, and I will die, and one day, even if we don't destroy it, the earth itself will die, the Holy endures, unfolding, always and everywhere.

LAST WORDS

Do not be daunted by the enormity of the world's grief.
Do justly, now. Love mercy, now. Walk humbly, now.
You are not obligated to complete the work,
but neither are you free to abandon it.

Adapted from the TALMUD

"All good things must come to an end," Mother used to intone whenever, as a small girl, I balked at leaving off some delightful activity or grieved at the departure of a favorite guest. Ours is a family given to truisms of this sort: handsome is as handsome does; it never rains but it pours; the apple never falls far from the tree; in the dark all cats are gray. These once maddened me, but now I can see that some do actually hint at cosmic truths. All things good and bad—life itself, that ultimate mixed blessing—must indeed come to an end. Our spiritual essence rests on this premise that we are transitory beings.

Even though Mother's bromide was meant as reassurance, partings have always panicked me. At four, I'm told, I resisted leaving Guam because my daddy had gone to heaven there and I would not abandon him. About to begin college, I penned in my diary: "But to leave, to say with finality, goodbye old life that I have always known, goodbye house, town, family, love—oh this is pain and panic and bewilderment far wilder than I have ever known." Over time, my feelings have lost their hysterical edge, but I continue to crave stasis and continuity in both my routine and my relationships. This morning when I went out, George had switched the places of two hibiscuses. I wasn't troubled by the change—but I noticed!

I remember being wrenched from my stolidity a few years ago by a series of circumstantial shifts. In a computer catastrophe of monstrous proportions, I lost eleven years of my writing life: the drafts of five books, innumerable reviews, business and personal correspondence, financial records, diaries and journals dating back to my fourteenth year. All these files existed in full in two different media, both of which failed me at once. More grievous yet was the departure of my daughter and her family to Denver for her husband's medical residency there. In more than thirty years, we'd sent Anne off many times, to a variety of destinations: summer camp; Honduras to vaccinate pigs against hog cholera; Smith College; the Peace Corps fisheries program in Zaire; a biochemistry lab in Madrid; Lugulu Friends Hospital in rural Kenya. I suppose we were lucky that she was remaining this time not only on the same continent but in the same time zone. Until then, however, Tucson had remained her permanent address and so she had somehow "belonged" here. No longer.

I wasn't suffering from empty-nest syndrome. Anne hadn't lived with us for fifteen years, and Matthew had been gone almost as long. I have never sighed, like my mother-in-law, "Life is never as good after the children have gone." In fact, partly as a result of watching my children strike off on their own, life has never been better. A saying I came across when they were little has stayed with me: "There are but two things we can give our children. One is roots, the other wings." Now that they've fledged, I don't want them back in the nest; they'd be too big for it.

Since we hadn't expected Anne to settle in Tucson, the eight years she lived here after returning from Africa were pure bounty. During them, we saw her complete a master's degree and Eric, medical school at the University of Arizona. We witnessed their marriage and the birth of their son, thrilling to his every wail and giggle. We logged hours playing bridge and watching basketball; took care of each other's dogs; exchanged gifts, recipes, advice, gossip, colds. We've continued to visit several times a year, first in Denver, then on the Zuni reservation, now in Gallup, New Mexico, as well as in Tucson, but the easy intimacy of neighbors ended and I mourned it.

In the essay called "Enough Is Enough," I advised never possessing anything you cannot bear to live without. This is sound enough counsel for the objects I had in mind, but it doesn't quite work for people, who are not possessions but companions in life's project and, once loved, can never be relinquished. I couldn't let Anne, Eric, and Colin go as I have a feather bush, a wicker basket. My father has been dead for more than fifty years, but I have never let him go. On the contrary, after Mother assured me that heaven was overhead wherever I went, I took him along, and he has flourished in my head and heart ever since, together now with my mother and stepfather, several other beloved relatives and friends, my foster-son, and an assortment of pets. My surviving children, separated only by distance and not by death, have simply joined them there. Thanks to them all, my awareness has stretched further than I could have anticipated.

"Between God and me there is no 'Between,'" the Christian mystic Meister Eckhart observed. Believing as I do that God is the Whole of It, that our every atom bears God into being, I cannot experience myself as truly apart. Between me and my children, my father, the little lizard skittering about my studio, the very first blossom on the young desert willow outside my door, there is no Between.

Just now, one more parting confronts me: from you, the readers who have kept me company throughout this book. Though I've met only a handful of you, I've chattered to all of you night and day as I composed these essays, since the amount of actual writing time and the number of words are always minuscule compared to the reflection and energy behind them. Your ghostly presence has helped me achieve focus at a time when my ideas have seemed, like my actions, especially scattered. I hope I've given you something in return. Between you and me there is no Between. Goodbye.

NOTES

First Words

1. Astute readers will note that, throughout this book, I quote from a variety of translations of the Bible, largely because I used the first one that came to hand but also because I don't believe that any one of them is more "the word of God" than are the others.

Left at the Altar

1. See Robert W. Funk, Roy W. Hoover, and the Jesus Seminar, eds., *The Five Gospels: The Search for the Authentic Words of Jesus; New Translation and Commentary* (New York: Macmillan, 1993), and Burton L. Mack, *The Lost Gospel: The Book of Q and Christian Origins* (San Francisco, Calif.: HarperSanFrancisco, 1993).
2. B. A. Robinson, "The Gospel of Q: The Gospel's Internal Structure," Ontario Consultants on Religious Tolerance, 1998, www.religioustolerance.org/gosp_q3.htm.
3. I used to think this substitution of "kindom" for "kingdom" sounded a little precious, but I have learned that what matters about a word is not how it sounds but whether it tells the truth. "Kingdom" means nothing to me, since I grew up under a different form of leadership and do not think of God as an entity outside of creation. But "kindom" means all the world to me, since it defines the relationship between me and the All to which I am intrinsic. Progressive Christians in a variety of denominations who are committed to articulating the social gospel coined and have used the word before me.
4. As Arizona State University professor Randel McCraw Helms avers in *Who Wrote the Gospels?* (Altadena, Calif.: Millennium Press, 1997).

5. Pope John Paul II, "Apostolic Letter *Ordinatio Sacerdotalis* on Reserving Priestly Ordination to Men Alone," May 22, 1994, the Solemnity of Pentecost.
6. In Marge Pellegrino, "Owl and Panther: Writing from the Darkness," *Tucson Weekly*, September 12, 2002.
7. United States Conference of Catholic Bishops, Catholic Campaign for Human Development, *Principles, Prophecy, and a Pastoral Response: An Overview of Modern Catholic Social Teaching*, Chapter 4, www.nccbuscc.org/cchd/ppprexcerpt.shtml.
8. This statement refers to "the international movement We Are Church, founded in Rome in 1996, committed to the renewal of the Roman Catholic Church on the basis of the Second Vatican Council (1962–1965) and the theological spirit developed from it," www.we-are-church.org. In the United States, Call to Action and several other organizations are linked to We Are Church.

Coveting the Saints: Our Lady of Guadalupe and the Soup

1. Philip E. Lampe, "Our Lady of Guadalupe: Victim of Prejudice or Ignorance?" *Listening: Journal of Religion and Culture* 21, no. 1 (1986), 9.
2. See James E. Fiedler, *Denver Catholic Register*, December 7, 1977.
3. J. T. Meehan, S.J., *Guadalupe Our Mother* (Washington, N.J.: Blue Army of Our Lady, 1970), 5.
4. Robert Feeney, *Mary, Mother of the Americas* (Ligouri, Mo.: Liguori Publications, 1984), 19.
5. Ibid., 21.
6. Harold J. Rahm, S.J., *Our Lady of Guadalupe*, pamphlet, no publishing information.
7. Meehan, *Guadalupe Our Mother*, 7–11.
8. According to Rahm, *Our Lady of Guadalupe*.
9. Miguel Leatham, "Indigenista Hermeneutics and the Historical Meaning of Our Lady of Guadalupe of Mexico," *Folklore Forum* 22, nos. 1/2, 30.
10. I have extracted these details from Fiedler and Leatham.
11. See Fiedler.
12. A term only residents of the United States would arrogate exclusively to themselves.

13. Lampe, "Our Lady of Guadalupe," 11, 12.

14. Quoted by Fiedler.

15. Benedict Carey, "Long-Awaited Medical Study Questions the Power of Prayer," *New York Times*, March 31, 2006.

16. I learned this apt phrase reflecting the systemic sources of poverty from the Reverend Delle McCormick, a UCC minister and the executive director of BorderLinks, a binational nonprofit organization that offers experiential educational seminars along the border focusing on the issues of global economics, militarization, immigration, and popular resistance to oppression and violence.

A Calling

1. *The Summa Theologica of St. Thomas Aquinas*, trans. Fathers of the English Dominican Province, 2nd and rev. ed (1920), www.newadvent .org/summa.

2. Note that the naughty little things are daughters, not sons—but that's a topic for another essay.

3. *The American Heritage Dictionary of the English Language*, 4th ed., s.v. "Discernment."

4. Valparaiso Project on the Education and Formation of People in Faith, "Discernment," www.practicingourfaith.org.

5. Benedictine Sisters of Perpetual Adoration, benedictinesisters.org.

Poor God

1. Barna Group, "Faith Commitment," 2006, www.barna.org/FlexPage .aspx?Page=Topic&TopicID=19.

2. Thomas Cleary, comp. and trans., *The Pocket Zen Reader* (Boston: Shambhala, 1999), quoted at www.beliefnet.com.

3. Quoted in Jeff Schmidt, *365 Buddha: Daily Meditations* (New York: Jeremy P. Tarcher/Putnam, 2002), and at www.beliefnet.com.

God in Love

1. www.jesus-is-lord.com.

2. Many fundamentalists fixate on this "authorized" version as the in-

errant Word of God, even asserting that subsequent translations do the work of Satan. Although I grew up with the King James Version and feel a special fondness for it (as must every student of English literature, whether a believer or not), I cannot imagine what qualifies it, and it alone, as divine utterance, still less why its singularity matters. My bafflement cannot be attributed to a lack of instruction, since people seem happy enough to harangue me, either verbally or in print, as though their lives depended on it. I do not believe that mine does.

3. Richard C. Lewontin, "The Wars over Evolution," *New York Review of Books* 52, no. 16, October 20, 2005.

4. *The Works of Jonathan Edwards* (New York: Garland, 1987), Vol. 2. Online at Christian Classics Ethereal Library, www.ccel.org/ccel/edwards/works2.html.

5. Authorship is uncertain, but the first seven rules are often attributed to J. Kent Ashcraft.

6. Chögyam Trungpa, *Cutting Through Spiritual Materialism*, ed. John Baker and Marvin Casper (Berkeley, Calif.: Shambhala, 1973).

Enough Is Enough

1. Craig R. Smith, True Wealth Online, Chapter 4.4, "Risk and Reward," www.true-wealth.com.

2. Paul Krugman, "Always Low Wages. Always," *New York Times*, May 13, 2005.

Risen? Risen Indeed!

1. David Adams Leeming, *The World of Myth* (New York: Oxford University Press, 1990), quoted at www.dreamscape.com/morgana/umbriel.htm.

The End of the World

1. Shelley E. Taylor et al., "Biobehavioral Responses to Stress in Females: Tend-and-Befriend, not Fight-or-Flight," *Psychological Review* 107, no. 3 (2000), 411–29.

2. Daniel Goleman, interviewed by Moira Gunn, *Tech Nation*, National Public Radio, February 11, 2003.

3. Dr. Robert D. Crane, "Hirabah versus Jihad," Islamic Research Foundation International, Inc., www.irfi.org/articles/articles_301_350/hirabah_versus_jihad.htm.

4. Anisa Mehdi, "Rethinking the Word 'Jihad,' " *All Things Considered*, National Public Radio, January 7, 2005, www.npr.org/templates/story/story.php?storyId=4273847.

5. Molly Ivins, "The 'Long War'? Oh, Goody," *Boulder (Colo.) Daily Camera*, March 18, 2006.

6. Multiple sources say that the United States possesses more than ten thousand nuclear weapons and thousands of tons of chemical weapons but simply researches biological weapons for defense purposes, having ended its offensive biological program in 1969.

7. White House Press Release, February 5, 2003, www.whitehouse.gov.

8. Reported by the United Nations World Food Programme, www.wfp.org.